THE FUTURE OF AN ILLUSION

SIGMUND FREUD, the founder of psychoanalysis, was born in 1856 in Austria. From 1876 to 1882 he worked in the Physiological Institute and a hospital in Vienna, studying at the same time for his M.D., which he received in 1881. During this period he did research with Josef Breuer on the use of hypnosis in the treatment of hysteria and developed his first psychoanalytic hypotheses. In 1885 he went to Paris for a year of study with the famous neurologist, Charcot. When he returned to Vienna, he became lecturer in neuropathology and later professor at the university there. He remained in Vienna until the advent of the Nazis. He then fled to England, where he died in 1939.

Some of Freud's most famous and significant books are: *The Interpretation of Dreams* (1900), *On Dreams* (1901), *The Psychopathology of Everyday Life* (1904), *On Psychotherapy* (1905), *The Origin and Development of Psychoanalysis* (1909), *Totem and Taboo* (1913), and *Beyond the Pleasure Principle* (1920). After 1923 Freud wrote several less technical books in which he applied the psychoanalytic approach to the study of culture. One of these is THE FUTURE OF AN ILLUSION (1927). Others are *Civilization and Its Discontents* (1929) and *Moses and Monotheism* (1939).

A General Selection from the Works of Sigmund Freud edited by John Rickman and *The Life and Work of Sigmund Freud* by Ernest Jones, edited and abridged in one volume by Lionel Trilling and Steven Marcus, are available in Anchor Books.

1939
1856
———
83

SIGMUND FREUD

The Future of an Illusion

TRANSLATED BY

W. D. ROBSON-SCOTT

REVISED AND NEWLY EDITED BY

JAMES STRACHEY

ANCHOR BOOKS

DOUBLEDAY & COMPANY, INC.

GARDEN CITY, NEW YORK

The first edition of W. D. Robson-Scott's English translation of *Die Zukunft einer Illusion* (Vienna, 1927) was published by the Liveright Publishing Corporation in 1953 and by Anchor Books in 1957. The present edition of THE FUTURE OF AN ILLUSION is a completely revised and fully annotated version of that translation prepared under the general editorship of James Strachey, in collaboration with Anna Freud, and assisted by Alix Strachey and Alan Tyson, for *The Standard Edition of the Complete Psychological Works of Sigmund Freud*. It was originally published in 1961 by The Hogarth Press, London. A full Bibliography and Index have been added. This revised translation is published in Anchor Books by arrangement with the Liveright Publishing Corporation, which will publish a hardbound edition in the United States.

Revised Anchor Books edition: 1964

CONTENTS

EDITOR'S NOTE

GERMAN EDITIONS: *Die Zukunft einer Illusion*

1927   Leipzig, Vienna and Zurich: Internation-
        aler Psychoanalytischer Verlag. Pp. 91.
1928   2nd ed. Same publishers. (Unchanged.)
        Pp. 91.
1928   *G.S.*, **11**, 411–66.
1948   *G.W.*, **14**, 325–380.

ENGLISH TRANSLATION: *The Future of an Illusion*

1928   London: Hogarth Press and Institute of
        Psycho-Analysis. Pp. 98. (Tr. W. D.
        Robson-Scott.)
1961   *S.E.*, **21**, 3–56. (Largely modified version
        of above.)

The present translation is a corrected reprint of
the *Standard Edition* version.

This work was begun in the spring of 1927, it
was finished by September and published in No-
vember of the same year.

In the 'Postscript' which Freud added in 1935
to his *Autobiographical Study* he remarked on 'a
significant change' that had come about in his
writings during the previous decade. 'My interest',
he explained, 'after making a long *détour* through
the natural sciences, medicine and psychotherapy,

returned to the cultural problems which had fascinated me long before, when I was a youth scarcely old enough for thinking' (*Standard Ed.*, **20**, 72). He had, of course, touched several times on those problems in the intervening years—especially in *Totem and Taboo* (1912–13);[1] but it was with *The Future of an Illusion* that he entered on the series of studies which were to be his major concern for the remainder of his life. Of these the most important were *Civilization and Its Discontents* (1930*a*), which is the direct successor to the present work, the discussion of philosophies of life which forms the last of the *New Introductory Lectures* (1933*a*), *Why War?* (1933*b*), Freud's open letter to Einstein, and finally *Moses and Monotheism* (1939*a*), which he worked at from 1934 onwards.

In view of Freud's sweeping pronouncement on p. 2 ('I scorn to distinguish between culture and civilization') and of a similar remark towards the end of *'Why War?'*, it seems unnecessary to embark on the tiresome problem of the proper translation of the German word *'Kultur'*. We have usually, but not invariably, chosen 'civilization' for the noun and 'cultural' for the adjective.

Editorial additions, whether to the text or the footnotes, are printed in square brackets.

---

[1] His earliest published approach to the problem of religion was in the paper on 'Obsessive Actions and Religious Practices' (1907*b*).

THE FUTURE OF AN ILLUSION

I

WHEN one has lived for quite a long time in a particular civilization[1] and has often tried to discover what its origins were and along what path it has developed, one sometimes also feels tempted to take a glance in the other direction and to ask what further fate lies before it and what transformations it is destined to undergo. But one soon finds that the value of such an enquiry is diminished from the outset by several factors. Above all, because there are only a few people who can survey human activity in its full compass. Most people have been obliged to restrict themselves to a single, or a few, fields of it. But the less a man knows about the past and the present the more insecure must prove to be his judgement of the future. And there is the further difficulty that precisely in a judgement of this kind the subjective expectations of the individual play a part which it is difficult to assess; and these turn out to be dependent on purely personal factors in his own experience, on the greater or lesser optimism of his

---

[1] [See Editor's Note, p. ix.]

attitude to life, as it has been dictated for him by his temperament or by his success or failure. Finally, the curious fact makes itself felt that in general people experience their present naïvely, as it were, without being able to form an estimate of its contents; they have first to put themselves at a distance from it—the present, that is to say, must have become the past—before it can yield points of vantage from which to judge the future.

Thus anyone who gives way to the temptation to deliver an opinion on the probable future of our civilization will do well to remind himself of the difficulties I have just pointed out, as well as of the uncertainty that attaches quite generally to any prophecy. It follows from this, so far as I am concerned, that I shall make a hasty retreat before a task that is too great, and shall promptly seek out the small tract of territory which has claimed my attention hitherto, as soon as I have determined its position in the general scheme of things.

Human civilization, by which I mean all those respects in which human life has raised itself above its animal status and differs from the life of beasts—and I scorn to distinguish between culture and civilization—, presents, as we know, two aspects to the observer. It includes on the one hand all the knowledge and capacity that men have acquired in order to control the forces of nature and extract its wealth for the satisfaction of human needs, and, on the other hand, all the regulations necessary in order to adjust the relations of men to one another and especially the distribution of the available wealth. The two trends of civilization are not independent of each other: firstly, because the mutual relations of men are profoundly influenced by the amount of instinctual satisfaction which the existing wealth makes possible; secondly, because an individual man can himself come to function as wealth in relation to another one, in so far as the other person makes use of his capacity for work, or chooses him as a sexual object; and thirdly, moreover, because every individual is virtually an enemy of civilization, though civilization is supposed to be an object of universal human interest.[2] It is remarkable that, little as men are able to exist in isolation, they should nevertheless feel as a heavy burden the sacrifices which civilization expects of them in order to make a communal life possible. Thus civilization has to be defended against the individual, and its regulations, institutions and commands are directed to that task. They aim not only at effecting a certain distribution of wealth but at maintaining that distribution; indeed, they have to protect everything that contributes to the con-

[2] [The hostility of human individuals to civilization plays a large part in the earlier chapters of this work. Freud returned to the subject and discussed it still more fully two years later in his *Civilization and Its Discontents* (1930a).]

quest of nature and the production of wealth against men's hostile impulses. Human creations are easily destroyed, and science and technology, which have built them up, can also be used for their annihilation.

One thus gets an impression that civilization is something which was imposed on a resisting majority by a minority which understood how to obtain possession of the means to power and coercion. It is, of course, natural to assume that these difficulties are not inherent in the nature of civilization itself but are determined by the imperfections of the cultural forms which have so far been developed. And in fact it is not difficult to indicate those defects. While mankind has made continual advances in its control over nature and may expect to make still greater ones, it is not possible to establish with certainty that a similar advance has been made in the management of human affairs; and probably at all periods, just as now once again, many people have asked themselves whether what little civilization has thus acquired is indeed worth defending at all. One would think that a re-ordering of human relations should be possible, which would remove the sources of dissatisfaction with civilization by renouncing coercion and the suppression of the instincts, so that, undisturbed by internal discord, men might devote themselves to the acquisition of wealth and its enjoyment. That would be the golden age, but it is questionable if such a state of affairs can be realized. It seems rather that every civilization must be built up on coercion and renunciation of instinct; it does not even seem certain that if coercion were to cease the majority of human beings would be prepared to undertake to perform the work necessary for acquiring new wealth. One has, I think, to reckon with the fact that there are present in all men destructive, and therefore anti-social and anti-cultural, trends and that in a great number of people these are strong enough to determine their behaviour in human society.

This psychological fact has a decisive importance for our judgement of human civilization. Whereas we might at first think that its essence lies in controlling nature for the purpose of acquiring wealth and that the dangers which threaten it could be eliminated through a suitable distribution of that wealth among men, it now seems that the emphasis has moved over from the material to the mental. The decisive question is whether and to what extent it is possible to lessen the burden of the instinctual sacrifices imposed on men, to reconcile men to those which must necessarily remain and to provide a compensation for them. It is just as impossible to do without control of the mass[3] by a minority as it is to dispense with coer-

---

[3] ['*Masse.*' The German word has a very wide meaning. It is translated 'group' for special reasons in Freud's *Group Psychology* (1921c). See *S.E.,* **18,** 69 *n; I.P.L.,* **6,** 1 *n.* Here 'mass' seems more appropriate.]

cion in the work of civilization. For masses are lazy and unintelligent; they have no love for instinctual renunciation, and they are not to be convinced by argument of its inevitability; and the individuals composing them support one another in giving free rein to their indiscipline. It is only through the influence of individuals who can set an example and whom masses recognize as their leaders that they can be induced to perform the work and undergo the renunciations on which the existence of civilization depends. All is well if these leaders are persons who possess superior insight into the necessities of life and who have risen to the height of mastering their own instinctual wishes. But there is a danger that in order not to lose their influence they may give way to the mass more than it gives way to them, and it therefore seems necessary that they shall be independent of the mass by having means to power at their disposal. To put it briefly, there are two widespread human characteristics which are responsible for the fact that the regulations of civilization can only be maintained by a certain degree of coercion —namely, that men are not spontaneously fond of work and that arguments are of no avail against their passions.

I know the objections which will be raised against these assertions. It will be said that the characteristic of human masses depicted here, which is supposed to prove that coercion cannot be dispensed with in the work of civilization, is itself only the result of defects in the cultural regulations, owing to which men have become embittered, revengeful and inaccessible. New generations, who have been brought up in kindness and taught to have a high opinion of reason, and who have experienced the benefits of civilization at an early age, will have a different attitude to it. They will feel it as a possession of their very own and will be ready for its sake to make the sacrifices as regards work and instinctual satisfaction that are necessary for its preservation. They will be able to do without coercion and will differ little from their leaders. If no culture has so far produced human masses of such a quality, it is because no culture has yet devised regulations which will influence men in this way, and in particular from childhood onwards.

It may be doubted whether it is possible at all, or at any rate as yet, at the present stage of our control over nature, to set up cultural regulations of this kind. It may be asked where the number of superior, unswerving and disinterested leaders are to come from who are to act as educators of the future generations, and it may be alarming to think of the enormous amount of coercion that will inevitably be required before these intentions can be carried out. The grandeur of the plan and its importance for the future of human civilization cannot be disputed. It is securely based on the psychological discovery that man is equipped with the most varied instinctual dispositions, whose ultimate course is determined by the experiences of early childhood. But for the same reason the limitations of man's capacity for education set bounds to the effectiveness of such a transformation in his culture. One may question whether, and in what degree, it would be possible for a different cultural environment to do away with the two characteristics of human masses which make the guidance of human affairs so difficult. The experiment has not yet been made. Probably a certain percentage of mankind (owing to a pathological disposition or an excess of instinctual strength) will always remain asocial; but if it were feasible merely to reduce the majority that is hostile towards civilization to-day into a minority, a great deal would have been accomplished—perhaps all that *can* be accomplished.

I should not like to give the impression that I have strayed a long way from the line laid down for my enquiry [p. 1]. Let me therefore give an express assurance that I have not the least intention of making judgements on the great experiment in civilization that is now in progress in the vast country that stretches between Europe and Asia.[4] I have neither the special knowledge nor

[4] [See, however, some remarks in Chapter V of *Civilization and Its Discontents* (1930a), *S.E.*, **21**, 112 ff., and at two points in *Why War?* (1933b) and a long discussion in the last of the *New Introductory Lectures* (1933a).]

the capacity to decide on its practicability, to test the expediency of the methods employed or to measure the width of the inevitable gap between intention and execution. What is in preparation there is unfinished and therefore eludes an investigation for which our own long-consolidated civilization affords us material.

II

WE have slipped unawares out of the economic field into the field of psychology. At first we were tempted to look for the assets of civilization in the available wealth and in the regulations for its distribution. But with the recognition that every civilization rests on a compulsion to work and a renunciation of instinct and therefore inevitably provokes opposition from those affected by these demands, it has become clear that civilization cannot consist principally or solely in wealth itself and the means of acquiring it and the arrangements for its distribution; for these things are threatened by the rebelliousness and destructive mania of the participants in civilization. Alongside of wealth we now come upon the means by which civilization can be defended—measures of coercion and other measures that are intended to reconcile men to it and to recompense them for their sacrifices. These latter may be described as the mental assets of civilization.

For the sake of a uniform terminology we will describe the fact that an instinct cannot be satis-

fied as a 'frustration', the regulation by which this
frustration is established as a 'prohibition' and
the condition which is produced by the prohibition as a 'privation'. The first step is to distinguish between privations which affect everyone
and privations which do not affect everyone but
only groups, classes or even single individuals.
The former are the earliest; with the prohibitions
that established them, civilization—who knows
how many thousands of years ago?—began to de-
tach man from his primordial animal condition.
We have found to our surprise that these privations are still operative and still form the kernel
of hostility to civilization. The instinctual wishes
that suffer under them are born afresh with every
child; there is a class of people, the neurotics, who
already react to these frustrations with asocial
behaviour. Among these instinctual wishes are
those of incest, cannibalism and lust for killing.
It sounds strange to place alongside one another
wishes which everyone seems united in repudiat-
ing and others about which there is so much lively
dispute in our civilization as to whether they shall
be permitted or frustrated; but psychologically it
is justifiable to do so. Nor is the attitude of civilization to these oldest instinctual wishes by any
means uniform. Cannibalism alone seems to be
universally proscribed and—to the non-psycho-
analytic view—to have been completely surmounted. The strength of the incestuous wishes

can still be detected behind the prohibition against
them; and under certain conditions killing is still
practised, and indeed commanded, by our civilization. It is possible that cultural developments
lie ahead of us in which the satisfaction of yet
other wishes, which are entirely permissible to-
day, will appear just as unacceptable as cannibalism does now.

These earliest instinctual renunciations already
involve a psychological factor which remains important for all further instinctual renunciations
as well. It is not true that the human mind has
undergone no development since the earliest times
and that, in contrast to the advances of science
and technology, it is the same to-day as it was at
the beginning of history. We can point out one of
these mental advances at once. It is in keeping
with the course of human development that external coercion gradually becomes internalized;
for a special mental agency, man's super-ego, takes
it over and includes it among its commandments.[1]
Every child presents this process of transformation to us; only by that means does it become a
moral and social being. Such a strengthening of
the super-ego is a most precious cultural asset in
the psychological field. Those in whom it has
taken place are turned from being opponents of
civilization into being its vehicles. The greater

[1] [See Chapter III of *The Ego and the Id* (1923*b*),
Standard Ed., **19**, 28 ff.; *I.P.L.*, **12**, 18 ff.]

their number is in a cultural unit the more secure is its culture and the more it can dispense with external measures of coercion. Now the degree of this internalization differs greatly between the various instinctual prohibitions. As regards the earliest cultural demands, which I have mentioned, the internalization seems to have been very extensively achieved, if we leave out of account the unwelcome exception of the neurotics. But the case is altered when we turn to the other instinctual claims. Here we observe with surprise and concern that a majority of people obey the cultural prohibitions on these points only under the pressure of external coercion—that is, only where that coercion can make itself effective and so long as it is to be feared. This is also true of what are known as the *moral* demands of civilization, which likewise apply to everyone. Most of one's experiences of man's moral untrustworthiness fall into this category. There are countless civilized people who would shrink from murder or incest but who do not deny themselves the satisfaction of their avarice, their aggressive urges or their sexual lusts, and who do not hesitate to injure other people by lies, fraud and calumny, so long as they can remain unpunished for it; and this, no doubt, has always been so through many ages of civilization.

If we turn to those restrictions that apply only to certain classes of society, we meet with a state of things which is flagrant and which has always been recognized. It is to be expected that these underprivileged classes will envy the favoured ones their privileges and will do all they can to free themselves from their own surplus of privation. Where this is not possible, a permanent measure of discontent will persist within the culture concerned and this can lead to dangerous revolts. If, however, a culture has not got beyond a point at which the satisfaction of one portion of its participants depends upon the suppression of another, and perhaps larger, portion—and this is the case in all present-day cultures—it is understandable that the suppressed people should develop an intense hostility towards a culture whose existence they make possible by their work, but in whose wealth they have too small a share. In such conditions an internalization of the cultural prohibitions among the suppressed people is not to be expected. On the contrary, they are not prepared to acknowledge the prohibitions, they are intent on destroying the culture itself, and possibly even on doing away with the postulates on which it is based. The hostility of these classes to civilization is so obvious that it has caused the more latent hostility of the social strata that are better provided for to be overlooked. It goes without saying that a civilization which leaves so large a number of its participants unsatisfied and drives them into revolt neither has nor deserves the prospect of a lasting existence.

The extent to which a civilization's precepts have been internalized—to express it popularly and unpsychologically: the moral level of its participants—is not the only form of mental wealth that comes into consideration in estimating a civilization's value. There are in addition its assets in the shape of ideals and artistic creations—that is, the satisfactions that can be derived from those sources.

People will be only too readily inclined to include among the psychical assets of a culture its ideals—its estimates of what achievements are the highest and the most to be striven after. It will seem at first as though these ideals would determine the achievements of the cultural unit; but the actual course of events would appear to be that the ideals are based on the first achievements which have been made possible by a combination of the culture's internal gifts and external circumstances, and that these first achievements are then held on to by the ideal as something to be carried further. The satisfaction which the ideal offers to the participants in the culture is thus of a narcissistic nature; it rests on their pride in what has already been successfully achieved. To make this satisfaction complete calls for a comparison with other cultures which have aimed at different achievements and have developed different ideals.

On the strength of these differences every culture claims the right to look down on the rest. In this way cultural ideals become a source of discord and enmity between different cultural units, as can be seen most clearly in the case of nations.

The narcissistic satisfaction provided by the cultural ideal is also among the forces which are successful in combating the hostility to culture within the cultural unit. This satisfaction can be shared in not only by the favoured classes, which enjoy the benefits of the culture, but also by the suppressed ones, since the right to despise the people outside it compensates them for the wrongs they suffer within their own unit. No doubt one is a wretched plebeian, harassed by debts and military service; but, to make up for it, one is a Roman citizen, one has one's share in the task of ruling other nations and dictating their laws. This identification of the suppressed classes with the class who rules and exploits them is, however, only part of a larger whole. For, on the other hand, the suppressed classes can be emotionally attached to their masters; in spite of their hostility to them they may see in them their ideals; unless such relations of a fundamentally satisfying kind subsisted, it would be impossible to understand how a number of civilizations have survived so long in spite of the justifiable hostility of large human masses.

A different kind of satisfaction is afforded by

art to the participants in a cultural unit, though as a rule it remains inaccessible to the masses, who are engaged in exhausting work and have not enjoyed any personal education. As we discovered long since,[2] art offers substitutive satisfactions for the oldest and still most deeply felt cultural renunciations, and for that reason it serves as nothing else does to reconcile a man to the sacrifices he has made on behalf of civilization. On the other hand, the creations of art heighten his feelings of identification, of which every cultural unit stands in so much need, by providing an occasion for sharing highly valued emotional experiences. And when those creations picture the achievements of his particular culture and bring to his mind its ideals in an impressive manner, they also minister to his narcissistic satisfaction.

No mention has yet been made of what is perhaps the most important item in the psychical inventory of a civilization. This consists in its religious ideas in the widest sense—in other words (which will be justified later) in its illusions.

[2] [Cf., for instance, 'Creative Writers and Day-Dreaming' (1908e).]

III

In what does the peculiar value of religious ideas lie?

We have spoken of the hostility to civilization which is produced by the pressure that civilization exercises, the renunciations of instinct which it demands. If one imagines its prohibitions lifted —if, then, one may take any woman one pleases as a sexual object, if one may without hesitation kill one's rival for her love or anyone else who stands in one's way, if, too, one can carry off any of the other man's belongings without asking leave—how splendid, what a string of satisfactions one's life would be! True, one soon comes across the first difficulty: everyone else has exactly the same wishes as I have and will treat me with no more consideration than I treat him. And so in reality only one person could be made unrestrictedly happy by such a removal of the restrictions of civilization, and he would be a tyrant, a dictator, who had seized all the means to power. And even he would have every reason to wish that the others would observe at least one cultural commandment: 'thou shalt not kill'.

But how ungrateful, how short-sighted after all, to strive for the abolition of civilization! What would then remain would be a state of nature, and that would be far harder to bear. It is true that nature would not demand any restrictions of instinct from us, she would let us do as we liked; but she has her own particularly effective method of restricting us. She destroys us—coldly, cruelly, relentlessly, as it seems to us, and possibly through the very things that occasioned our satisfaction. It was precisely because of these dangers with which nature threatens us that we came together and created civilization, which is also, among other things, intended to make our communal life possible. For the principal task of civilization, its actual *raison d'être,* is to defend us against nature.

We all know that in many ways civilization does this fairly well already, and clearly as time goes on it will do it much better. But no one is under the illusion that nature has already been vanquished; and few dare hope that she will ever be entirely subjected to man. There are the elements, which seem to mock at all human control: the earth, which quakes and is torn apart and buries all human life and its works; water, which deluges and drowns everything in a turmoil; storms, which blow everything before them; there are diseases, which we have only recently recognized as attacks by other organisms; and finally there is the painful riddle of death, against which no medicine has yet been found, nor probably will be. With these forces nature rises up against us, majestic, cruel and inexorable; she brings to our mind once more our weakness and helplessness, which we thought to escape through the work of civilization. One of the few gratifying and exalting impressions which mankind can offer is when, in the face of an elemental catastrophe, it forgets the discordancies of its civilization and all its internal difficulties and animosities, and recalls the great common task of preserving itself against the superior power of nature.

For the individual, too, life is hard to bear, just as it is for mankind in general. The civilization in which he participates imposes some amount of privation on him, and other men bring him a measure of suffering, either in spite of the precepts of his civilization or because of its imperfections. To this are added the injuries which untamed nature—he calls it Fate—inflicts on him. One might suppose that this condition of things would result in a permanent state of anxious expectation in him and a severe injury to his natural narcissism. We know already how the individual reacts to the injuries which civilization and other men inflict on him: he develops a corresponding degree of resistance to the regulations of civilization and of hostility to it. But how does he defend himself against the superior powers of nature, of Fate, which threaten him as they threaten all the rest?

Civilization relieves him of this task; it performs it in the same way for all alike; and it is noteworthy that in this almost all civilizations act alike. Civilization does not call a halt in the task of defending man against nature, it merely pursues it by other means. The task is a manifold one. Man's self-regard, seriously menaced, calls for consolation; life and the universe must be robbed of their terrors; moreover his curiosity, moved, it is true, by the strongest practical interest, demands an answer.

A great deal is already gained with the first step: the humanization of nature. Impersonal forces and destinies cannot be approached; they remain eternally remote. But if the elements have passions that rage as they do in our own souls, if death itself is not something spontaneous but the violent act of an evil Will, if everywhere in nature there are Beings around us of a kind that we know in our own society, then we can breathe freely, can feel at home in the uncanny and can deal by psychical means with our senseless anxiety. We are still defenceless, perhaps, but we are no longer helplessly paralysed; we can at least react. Perhaps, indeed, we are not even defenceless. We can apply the same methods against these violent supermen outside that we employ in our own society; we can try to adjure them, to appease them, to bribe them, and, by so influencing them, we may rob them of a part of their power. A replacement like this of natural science by psychology not only provides immediate relief, but also points the way to a further mastering of the situation.

For this situation is nothing new. It has an infantile prototype, of which it is in fact only the continuation. For once before one has found oneself in a similar state of helplessness: as a small child, in relation to one's parents. One had reason to fear them, and especially one's father; and yet one was sure of his protection against the dangers one knew. Thus it was natural to assimilate the two situations. Here, too, wishing played its part, as it does in dream-life. The sleeper may be seized with a presentiment of death, which threatens to place him in the grave. But the dream-work knows how to select a condition that will turn even that dreaded event into a wish-fulfilment: the dreamer sees himself in an ancient Etruscan grave which he has climbed down into, happy to find his archaeological interests satisfied.[1] In the same way, a man makes the forces of nature not simply into persons with whom he can associate as he would with his equals—that would

---

[1] [This was an actual dream of Freud's, reported in Chapter VI (G) of *The Interpretation of Dreams* (1900*a*), *Standard Ed.*, **5**, 454–5.]

not do justice to the overpowering impression which those forces make on him—but he gives them the character of a father. He turns them into gods, following in this, as I have tried to show,[2] not only an infantile prototype but a phylogenetic one.

In the course of time the first observations were made of regularity and conformity to law in natural phenomena, and with this the forces of nature lost their human traits. But man's helplessness remains and along with it his longing for his father, and the gods. The gods retain their threefold task: they must exorcize the terrors of nature, they must reconcile men to the cruelty of Fate, particularly as it is shown in death, and they must compensate them for the sufferings and privations which a civilized life in common has imposed on them.

But within these functions there is a gradual displacement of accent. It was observed that the phenomena of nature developed automatically according to internal necessities. Without doubt the gods were the lords of nature; they had arranged it to be as it was and now they could leave it to itself. Only occasionally, in what are known as miracles, did they intervene in its course, as though to make it plain that they had relinquished nothing of their original sphere of power. As re-

[2] [See Section 6 of the fourth essay in *Totem and Taboo* (1912–13), *Standard Ed.*, **13,** 146 ff.]

gards the apportioning of destinies, an unpleasant suspicion persisted that the perplexity and helplessness of the human race could not be remedied. It was here that the gods were most apt to fail. If they themselves created Fate, then their counsels must be deemed inscrutable. The notion dawned on the most gifted people of antiquity that Moira [Fate] stood above the gods and that the gods themselves had their own destinies. And the more autonomous nature became and the more the gods withdrew from it, the more earnestly were all expectations directed to the third function of the gods—the more did morality become their true domain. It now became the task of the gods to even out the defects and evils of civilization, to attend to the sufferings which men inflict on one another in their life together and to watch over the fulfilment of the precepts of civilization, which men obey so imperfectly. Those precepts themselves were credited with a divine origin; they were elevated beyond human society and were extended to nature and the universe.

And thus a store of ideas is created, born from man's need to make his helplessness tolerable and built up from the material of memories of the helplessness of his own childhood and the childhood of the human race. It can clearly be seen that the possession of these ideas protects him in two directions—against the dangers of nature and Fate, and against the injuries that threaten him from human society itself. Here is the gist of the matter. Life in this world serves a higher purpose; no doubt it is not easy to guess what that purpose is, but it certainly signifies a perfecting of man's nature. It is probably the spiritual part of man, the soul, which in the course of time has so slowly and unwillingly detached itself from the body, that is the object of this elevation and exaltation. Everything that happens in this world is an expression of the intentions of an intelligence superior to us, which in the end, though its ways and byways are difficult to follow, orders everything for the best—that is, to make it enjoyable for us. Over each one of us there watches a benevolent Providence which is only seemingly stern and which will not suffer us to become a plaything of the over-mighty and pitiless forces of nature. Death itself is not extinction, is not a return to inorganic lifelessness, but the beginning of a new kind of existence which lies on the path of development to something higher. And, looking in the other direction, this view announces that the same moral laws which our civilizations have set up govern the whole universe as well, except that they are maintained by a supreme court of justice with incomparably more power and consistency. In the end all good is rewarded and all evil punished, if not actually in this form of life then in the later existences that begin after death. In this way all the terrors, the sufferings and the hardships of life are destined to be obliterated. Life after death, which continues life on earth just as the invisible part of the spectrum joins on to the visible part, brings us all the perfection that we may perhaps have missed here. And the superior wisdom which directs this course of things, the infinite goodness that expresses itself in it, the justice that achieves its aim in it—these are the attributes of the divine beings who also created us and the world as a whole, or rather, of the one divine being into which, in our civilization, all the gods of antiquity have been condensed. The people which first succeeded in thus concentrating the divine attributes was not a little proud of the advance. It had laid open to view the father who had all along been hidden behind every divine figure as its nucleus. Fundamentally this was a return to the historical beginnings of the idea of God. Now that God was a single person, man's relations to him could recover the intimacy and intensity of the child's relation to his father. But if one had done so much for one's father, one wanted to have a reward, or at least to be his only beloved child, his Chosen People. Very much later, pious America laid claim to being 'God's own Country'; and, as regards one of the shapes in which men worship the deity, the claim is undoubtedly valid.

The religious ideas that have been summarized above have of course passed through a long process of development and have been adhered to in various phases by various civilizations. I have singled out one such phase, which roughly corresponds to the final form taken by our present-day white Christian civilization. It is easy to see that not all the parts of this picture tally equally well with one another, that not all the questions that press for an answer receive one, and that it is difficult to dismiss the contradiction of daily experience. Nevertheless, such as they are, those ideas—ideas which are religious in the widest sense—are prized as the most precious possession of civilization, as the most precious thing it has to offer its participants. It is far more highly prized than all the devices for winning treasures from the earth or providing men with sustenance or preventing their illnesses, and so forth. People feel that life would not be tolerable if they did not attach to these ideas the value that is claimed for them. And now the question arises: what are these ideas in the light of psychology? Whence do they derive the esteem in which they are held? And, to take a further timid step, what is their real worth?

IV

AN enquiry which proceeds like a monologue, without interruption, is not altogether free from danger. One is too easily tempted into pushing aside thoughts which threaten to break into it, and in exchange one is left with a feeling of uncertainty which in the end one tries to keep down by over-decisiveness. I shall therefore imagine that I have an opponent who follows my arguments with mistrust, and here and there I shall allow him to interject some remarks.[1]

I hear him say: 'You have repeatedly used the expressions "civilization creates these religious ideas", "civilization places them at the disposal of its participants". There is something about this that sounds strange to me. I cannot myself say why, but it does not sound so natural as it does to say that civilization has made rules about

---

[1] [Freud had adopted the same method of presentation in his recent discussion of lay analysis (1926e) and also, though in somewhat different circumstances, a quarter of a century earlier in his paper on 'Screen Memories' (1899a).]

distributing the products of labour or about rights concerning women and children.'

I think, all the same, that I am justified in expressing myself in this way. I have tried to show that religious ideas have arisen from the same need as have all the other achievements of civilization: from the necessity of defending oneself against the crushingly superior force of nature. To this a second motive was added—the urge to rectify the shortcomings of civilization which made themselves painfully felt. Moreover, it is especially apposite to say that civilization gives the individual these ideas, for he finds them there already; they are presented to him ready-made, and he would not be able to discover them for himself. What he is entering into is the heritage of many generations, and he takes it over as he does the multiplication table, geometry, and similar things. There is indeed a difference in this, but that difference lies elsewhere and I cannot examine it yet. The feeling of strangeness that you mention may be partly due to the fact that this body of religious ideas is usually put forward as a divine revelation. But this presentation of it is itself a part of the religious system, and it entirely ignores the known historical development of these ideas and their differences in different epochs and civilizations.

'Here is another point, which seems to me to be more important. You argue that the humaniza-

tion of nature is derived from the need to put an
end to man's perplexity and helplessness in the
face of its dreaded forces, to get into a relation
with them and finally to influence them. But a
motive of this kind seems superfluous. Primitive
man has no choice, he has no other way of thinking. It is natural to him, something innate, as it
were, to project his existence outwards into the
world and to regard every event which he ob-
serves as the manifestation of beings who at bottom are like himself. It is his only method of com-
prehension. And it is by no means self-evident,
on the contrary it is a remarkable coincidence,
if by thus indulging his natural disposition he
succeeds in satisfying one of his greatest needs.'

I do not find that so striking. Do you suppose
that human thought has no practical motives, that
it is simply the expression of a disinterested curiosity? That is surely very improbable. I believe
rather that when man personifies the forces of
nature he is again following an infantile model.
He has learnt from the persons in his earliest environment that the way to influence them is to
establish a relation with them; and so, later on,
with the same end in view, he treats everything
else that he comes across in the same way as he
treated those persons. Thus I do not contradict
your descriptive observation; it is in fact natural
to man to personify everything that he wants to
understand in order later to control it (psychical

mastering as a preparation for physical mastering); but I provide in addition a motive and a
genesis for this peculiarity of human thinking.

'And now here is yet a third point. You have
dealt with the origin of religion once before, in
your book *Totem and Taboo* [1912–13]. But
there it appeared in a different light. Everything
was the son–father relationship. God was the ex-
alted father, and the longing for the father was the
root of the need for religion. Since then, it seems,
you have discovered the factor of human weakness and helplessness, to which indeed the chief
role in the formation of religion is generally as-
signed, and now you transpose everything that
was once the father complex into terms of helplessness. May I ask you to explain this transformation?'

With pleasure. I was only waiting for this in-
vitation. But is it really a transformation? In
Totem and Taboo it was not my purpose to explain the origin of religions but only of totemism.
Can you, from any of the views known to you,
explain the fact that the first shape in which the
protecting deity revealed itself to men should have
been that of an animal, that there was a prohibition against killing and eating this animal and
that nevertheless the solemn custom was to kill
and eat it communally once a year? This is precisely what happens in totemism. And it is hardly
to the purpose to argue about whether totemism

ought to be called a religion. It has intimate connections with the later god-religions. The totem
animals become the sacred animals of the gods;
and the earliest, but most fundamental moral
restrictions—the prohibitions against murder and
incest—originate in totemism. Whether or not
you accept the conclusions of *Totem and Taboo,*
I hope you will admit that a number of very remarkable, disconnected facts are brought together
in it into a consistent whole.

The question of why in the long run the animal
god did not suffice, and was replaced by a human
one, was hardly touched on in *Totem and Taboo,*
and other problems concerning the formation of
religion were not mentioned in the book at all.
Do you regard a limitation of that kind as the
same thing as a denial? My work is a good example of the strict isolation of the particular contribution which psycho-analytic discussion can
make to the solution of the problem of religion.
If I am now trying to add the other, less deeply
concealed part, you should not accuse me of con-
tradicting myself, just as before you accused me
of being one-sided. It is, of course, my duty to
point out the connecting links between what I said
earlier and what I put forward now, between the
deeper and the manifest motives, between the
father-complex and man's helplessness and need
for protection.

These connections are not hard to find. They

consist in the relation of the child's helplessness to the helplessness of the adult which continues it. So that, as was to be expected, the motives for the formation of religion which psycho-analysis revealed now turn out to be the same as the infantile contribution to the *manifest* motives. Let us transport ourselves into the mental life of a child. You remember the choice of object according to the anaclitic [attachment] type, which psycho-analysis talks of?[2] The libido there follows the paths of narcissistic needs and attaches itself to the objects which ensure the satisfaction of those needs. In this way the mother, who satisfies the child's hunger, becomes its first love-object and certainly also its first protection against all the undefined dangers which threaten it in the external world—its first protection against anxiety, we may say.

In this function [of protection] the mother is soon replaced by the stronger father, who retains that position for the rest of childhood. But the child's attitude to its father is coloured by a peculiar ambivalence. The father himself constitutes a danger for the child, perhaps because of its earlier relation to its mother. Thus it fears him no less than it longs for him and admires him. The indications of this ambivalence in the attitude to the father are deeply imprinted in every religion,

[2] [See Freud's paper on narcissism (1914c), *Standard Ed.*, **14,** 87.]

as was shown in *Totem and Taboo*. When the growing individual finds that he is destined to remain a child for ever, that he can never do without protection against strange superior powers, he lends those powers the features belonging to the figure of his father; he creates for himself the gods whom he dreads, whom he seeks to propitiate, and whom he nevertheless entrusts with his own protection. Thus his longing for a father is a motive identical with his need for protection against the consequences of his human weakness. The defence against childish helplessness is what lends its characteristic features to the adult's reaction to the helplessness which *he* has to acknowledge—a reaction which is precisely the formation of religion. But it is not my intention to enquire any further into the development of the idea of God; what we are concerned with here is the finished body of religious ideas as it is transmitted by civilization to the individual.

V

LET us now take up the thread of our enquiry.[1] What, then, is the psychological significance of religious ideas and under what heading are we to classify them? The question is not at all easy to answer immediately. After rejecting a number of formulations, we will take our stand on the following one. Religious ideas are teachings and assertions about facts and conditions of external (or internal) reality which tell one something one has not discovered for oneself and which lay claim to one's belief. Since they give us information about what is most important and interesting to us in life, they are particularly highly prized. Anyone who knows nothing of them is very ignorant; and anyone who has added them to his knowledge may consider himself much the richer.

There are, of course, many such teachings about the most various things in the world. Every school lesson is full of them. Let us take geography. We are told that the town of Constance lies

[1] [From the end of Chapter III.]

on the Bodensee.[2] A student song adds: 'if you don't believe it, go and see.' I happen to have been there and can confirm the fact that that lovely town lies on the shore of a wide stretch of water which all those who live round it call the Bodensee; and I am now completely convinced of the correctness of this geographical assertion. In this connection I am reminded of another, very remarkable, experience. I was already a man of mature years when I stood for the first time on the hill of the Acropolis in Athens, between the temple ruins, looking out over the blue sea. A feeling of astonishment mingled with my joy. It seemed to say: 'So it really *is* true, just as we learnt at school!' How shallow and weak must have been the belief I then acquired in the real truth of what I heard, if I could be so astonished now! But I will not lay too much stress on the significance of this experience; for my astonishment could have had another explanation, which did not occur to me at the time and which is of a wholly subjective nature and has to do with the special character of the place.[3]

All teachings like these, then, demand belief in their contents, but not without producing grounds

[2] [The German name for what we call the Lake of Constance.]

[3] [This had happened in 1904, when Freud was almost fifty. He wrote a full account of the episode in an open letter to Romain Rolland some ten years after the present work (1936a).]

for their claim. They are put forward as the epito-
mized result of a longer process of thought based
on observation and certainly also on inferences.
If anyone wants to go through this process himself
instead of accepting its result, they show him how
to set about it. Moreover, we are always in addition given the source of the knowledge con-
veyed by them, where that source is not self-
evident, as it is in the case of geographical
assertions. For instance, the earth is shaped like a
sphere; the proofs adduced for this are Foucault's
pendulum experiment,[4] the behaviour of the hori-
zon and the possibility of circumnavigating the
earth. Since it is impracticable, as everyone concerned realizes, to send every schoolchild on a
voyage round the world, we are satisfied with
letting what is taught at school be taken on trust;
but we know that the path to acquiring a personal
conviction remains open.

Let us try to apply the same test to the teachings of religion. When we ask on what their claim
to be believed is founded, we are met with three
answers, which harmonize remarkably badly with
one another. Firstly, these teachings deserve to
be believed because they were already believed
by our primal ancestors; secondly, we possess
proofs which have been handed down to us from
those same primaeval times; and thirdly, it is for-

---

[4] [J. B. L. Foucault (1819–68) demonstrated the diurnal
motion of the earth by means of a pendulum in 1851.]

bidden to raise the question of their authentication at all. In former days anything so presumptuous was visited with the severest penalties, and even to-day society looks askance at any attempt to raise the question again.

This third point is bound to rouse our strongest suspicions. After all, a prohibition like this can only be for one reason—that society is very well aware of the insecurity of the claim it makes on behalf of its religious doctrines. Otherwise it would certainly be very ready to put the necessary data at the disposal of anyone who wanted to arrive at conviction. This being so, it is with a feeling of mistrust which it is hard to allay that we pass on to an examination of the other two grounds of proof. We ought to believe because our forefathers believed. But these ancestors of ours were far more ignorant than we are. They believed in things we could not possibly accept to-day; and the possibility occurs to us that the doctrines of religion may belong to that class too. The proofs they have left us are set down in writings which themselves bear every mark of untrustworthiness. They are full of contradictions, revisions and falsifications, and where they speak of factual confirmations they are themselves unconfirmed. It does not help much to have it asserted that their wording, or even their content only, originates from divine revelation; for this assertion is itself one of the doctrines whose authenticity is under examination, and no proposition can be a proof of itself.

Thus we arrive at the singular conclusion that of all the information provided by our cultural assets it is precisely the elements which might be of the greatest importance to us and which have the task of solving the riddles of the universe and of reconciling us to the sufferings of life—it is precisely those elements that are the least well authenticated of any. We should not be able to bring ourselves to accept anything of so little concern to us as the fact that whales bear young instead of laying eggs, if it were not capable of better proof than this.

This state of affairs is in itself a very remarkable psychological problem. And let no one suppose that what I have said about the impossibility of proving the truth of religious doctrines contains anything new. It has been felt at all times—undoubtedly, too, by the ancestors who bequeathed us this legacy. Many of them probably nourished the same doubts as ours, but the pressure imposed on them was too strong for them to have dared to utter them. And since then countless people have been tormented by similar doubts, and have striven to suppress them, because they thought it was their duty to believe; many brilliant intellects have broken down over this conflict, and many characters have been impaired by the compromises with which they have tried to find a way out of it.

If all the evidence put forward for the authenticity of religious teachings originates in the past, it is natural to look round and see whether the present, about which it is easier to form judgements, may not also be able to furnish evidence of the sort. If by this means we could succeed in clearing even a single portion of the religious system from doubt, the whole of it would gain enormously in credibility. The proceedings of the spiritualists meet us at this point; they are convinced of the survival of the individual soul and they seek to demonstrate to us beyond doubt the truth of this one religious doctrine. Unfortunately they cannot succeed in refuting the fact that the appearance and utterances of their spirits are merely the products of their own mental activity. They have called up the spirits of the greatest men and of the most eminent thinkers, but all the pronouncements and information which they have received from them have been so foolish and so wretchedly meaningless that one can find nothing credible in them but the capacity of the spirits to adapt themselves to the circle of people who have conjured them up.

I must now mention two attempts that have been made—both of which convey the impression of being desperate efforts—to evade the problem. One, of a violent nature, is ancient; the other is subtle and modern. The first is the *'Credo quia absurdum'* of the early Father of the Church.[5] It maintains that religious doctrines are outside the jurisdiction of reason—are above reason. Their truth must be felt inwardly, and they need not be comprehended. But this *Credo* is only of interest as a self-confession. As an authoritative statement it has no binding force. Am I to be obliged to believe *every* absurdity? And if not, why this one in particular? There is no appeal to a court above that of reason. If the truth of religious doctrines is dependent on an inner experience which bears witness to that truth, what is one to do about the many people who do not have this rare experience? One may require every man to use the gift of reason which he possesses, but one cannot erect, on the basis of a motive that exists only for a very few, an obligation that shall apply to everyone. If one man has gained an unshakable conviction of the true reality of religious doctrines from a state of ecstasy which has deeply moved him, of what significance is that to others?

The second attempt is the one made by the philosophy of 'As if'. This asserts that our thought-activity includes a great number of hypotheses whose groundlessness and even absurdity we fully realize. They are called 'fictions', but for a variety of practical reasons we have to behave 'as if' we

[5] ['I believe because it is absurd.' This is attributed to Tertullian.]

believed in these fictions. This is the case with
religious doctrines because of their incomparable
importance for the maintenance of human society.[6] This line of argument is not far removed
from the *'Credo quia absurdum'*. But I think the
demand made by the 'As if' argument is one that
only a philosopher could put forward. A man
whose thinking is not influenced by the artifices
of philosophy will never be able to accept it; in
such a man's view, the admission that something
is absurd or contrary to reason leaves no more
to be said. It cannot be expected of him that precisely in treating his most important interests he
shall forgo the guarantees he requires for all his
ordinary activities. I am reminded of one of my
children who was distinguished at an early age by
a peculiarly marked matter-of-factness. When the
children were being told a fairy story and were lis-
tening to it with rapt attention, he would come up
and ask: 'Is that a true story?' When he was told
it was not, he would turn away with a look of dis-

[6] I hope I am not doing him an injustice if I take the
philosopher of 'As if' as the representative of a view
which is not foreign to other thinkers: 'We include as fictions not merely indifferent theoretical operations but
ideational constructs emanating from the noblest minds,
to which the noblest part of mankind cling and of which
they will not allow themselves to be deprived. Nor is it
our object so to deprive them—for as *practical fictions* we
leave them all intact; they perish only as *theoretical truths.'*
(Hans Vaihinger, 1922, 68 [C. K. Ogden's translation,
1924, 48–9].)

dain. We may expect that people will soon behave in the same way towards the fairy tales of religion, in spite of the advocacy of 'As if'.

But at present they still behave quite differently; and in past times religious ideas, in spite of their incontrovertible lack of authentication, have exercised the strongest possible influence on mankind. This is a fresh psychological problem. We must ask where the inner force of those doctrines lies and to what it is that they owe their efficacy, independent as it is of recognition by reason.

VI

I THINK we have prepared the way sufficiently for an answer to both these questions. It will be found if we turn our attention to the psychical origin of religious ideas. These, which are given out as teachings, are not precipitates of experience or end-results of thinking: they are illusions, fulfilments of the oldest, strongest and most urgent wishes of mankind. The secret of their strength lies in the strength of those wishes. As we already know, the terrifying impression of helplessness in childhood aroused the need for protection—for protection through love—which was provided by the father; and the recognition that this helplessness lasts throughout life made it necessary to cling to the existence of a father, but this time a more powerful one. Thus the benevolent rule of a divine Providence allays our fear of the dangers of life; the establishment of a moral world-order ensures the fulfilment of the demands of justice, which have so often remained unfulfilled in human civilization; and the prolongation of earthly existence in a future life provides the local and

temporal framework in which these wish-fulfilments shall take place. Answers to the riddles
that tempt the curiosity of man, such as how the
universe began or what the relation is between
body and mind, are developed in conformity with
the underlying assumptions of this system. It is an
enormous relief to the individual psyche if the
conflicts of its childhood arising from the father-
complex—conflicts which it has never wholly overcome—are removed from it and brought to a
solution which is universally accepted.

When I say that these things are all illusions,
I must define the meaning of the word. An illusion
is not the same thing as an error; nor is it necessarily an error. Aristotle's belief that vermin are
developed out of dung (a belief to which ignorant
people still cling) was an error; so was the belief
of a former generation of doctors that *tabes dor-
salis* is the result of sexual excess. It would be
incorrect to call these errors illusions. On the
other hand, it was an illusion of Columbus's that
he had discovered a new sea-route to the Indies.
The part played by his wish in this error is very
clear. One may describe as an illusion the assertion made by certain nationalists that the Indo-
Germanic race is the only one capable of civilization; or the belief, which was only destroyed by
psycho-analysis, that children are creatures without sexuality. What is characteristic of illusions
is that they are derived from human wishes. In this

respect they come near to psychiatric delusions. But they differ from them, too, apart from the more complicated structure of delusions. In the case of delusions, we emphasize as essential their being in contradiction with reality. Illusions need not necessarily be false—that is to say, unrealizable or in contradiction to reality. For instance, a middle-class girl may have the illusion that a prince will come and marry her. This is possible; and a few such cases have occurred. That the Messiah will come and found a golden age is much less likely. Whether one classifies this belief as an illusion or as something analogous to a delusion will depend on one's personal attitude. Examples of illusions which have proved true are not easy to find, but the illusion of the alchemists that all metals can be turned into gold might be one of them. The wish to have a great deal of gold, as much gold as possible, has, it is true, been a good deal damped by our present-day knowledge of the determinants of wealth, but chemistry no longer regards the transmutation of metals into gold as impossible. Thus we call a belief an illusion when a wish-fulfilment is a prominent factor in its motivation, and in doing so we disregard its relations to reality, just as the illusion itself sets no store by verification.

Having thus taken our bearings, let us return once more to the question of religious doctrines. We can now repeat that all of them are illusions and insusceptible of proof. No one can be compelled to think them true, to believe in them. Some of them are so improbable, so incompatible with everything we have laboriously discovered about the reality of the world, that we may compare them—if we pay proper regard to the psychological differences—to delusions. Of the reality value of most of them we cannot judge; just as they cannot be proved, so they cannot be refuted. We still know too little to make a critical approach to them. The riddles of the universe reveal themselves only slowly to our investigation; there are many questions to which science to-day can give no answer. But scientific work is the only road which can lead us to a knowledge of reality outside ourselves. It is once again merely an illusion to expect anything from intuition and introspection; they can give us nothing but particulars about our own mental life, which are hard to interpret, never any information about the questions which religious doctrine finds it so easy to answer. It would be insolent to let one's own arbitrary will step into the breach and, according to one's personal estimate, declare this or that part of the religious system to be less or more acceptable. Such questions are too momentous for that; they might be called too sacred.

At this point one must expect to meet with an objection. 'Well then, if even obdurate sceptics admit that the assertions of religion cannot be refuted by reason, why should I not believe in them, since they have so much on their side— tradition, the agreement of mankind, and all the consolations they offer?' Why not, indeed? Just as no one can be forced to believe, so no one can be forced to disbelieve. But do not let us be satisfied with deceiving ourselves that arguments like these take us along the road of correct think- ing. If ever there was a case of a lame excuse we have it here. Ignorance is ignorance; no right to believe anything can be derived from it. In other matters no sensible person will behave so irre- sponsibly or rest content with such feeble grounds for his opinions and for the line he takes. It is only in the highest and most sacred things that he allows himself to do so. In reality these are only attempts at pretending to oneself or to other peo- ple that one is still firmly attached to religion, when one has long since cut oneself loose from it. Where questions of religion are concerned, people are guilty of every possible sort of dis- honesty and intellectual misdemeanour. Philoso- phers stretch the meaning of words until they retain scarcely anything of their original sense. They give the name of 'God' to some vague ab- straction which they have created for themselves; having done so they can pose before all the world as deists, as believers in God, and they can even boast that they have recognized a higher, purer concept of God, notwithstanding that their God is now nothing more than an insubstantial shadow and no longer the mighty personality of religious doctrines. Critics persist in describing as 'deeply religious' anyone who admits to a sense of man's insignificance or impotence in the face of the universe, although what constitutes the essence of the religious attitude is not this feeling but only the next step after it, the reaction to it which seeks a remedy for it. The man who goes no further, but humbly acquiesces in the small part which human beings play in the great world—such a man is, on the contrary, irreligious in the truest sense of the word.

To assess the truth-value of religious doctrines does not lie within the scope of the present enquiry. It is enough for us that we have recognized them as being, in their psychological nature, illusions. But we do not have to conceal the fact that this discovery also strongly influences our attitude to the question which must appear to many to be the most important of all. We know approximately at what periods and by what kind of men religious doctrines were created. If in addition we discover the motives which led to this, our attitude to the problem of religion will undergo a marked displacement. We shall tell ourselves that it would be very nice if there were a God who created the world and was a benevolent Providence, and if there were a moral order in the universe and an after-life; but it is a very striking fact that all this is exactly as we are bound to wish it to be. And it would be more remarkable still if our wretched, ignorant and downtrodden ancestors had succeeded in solving all these difficult riddles of the universe.

VII

HAVING recognized religious doctrines as illusions, we are at once faced by a further question: may not other cultural assets of which we hold a high opinion and by which we let our lives be ruled be of a similar nature? Must not the assumptions that determine our political regulations be called illusions as well? and is it not the case that in our civilization the relations between the sexes are disturbed by an erotic illusion or a number of such illusions? And once our suspicion has been aroused, we shall not shrink from asking too whether our conviction that we can learn something about external reality through the use of observation and reasoning in scientific work— whether this conviction has any better foundation. Nothing ought to keep us from directing our observation to our own selves or from applying our thought to criticism of itself. In this field a number of investigations open out before us, whose results could not but be decisive for the construction of a 'Weltanschauung'. We surmise, moreover, that such an effort would not be wasted and that it would at least in part justify our suspicion. But the author does not dispose of the means for undertaking so comprehensive a task; he needs must confine his work to following out one only of these illusions—that, namely, of religion.

But now the loud voice of our opponent brings us to a halt. We are called to account for our wrong-doing:

'Archaeological interests are no doubt most praiseworthy, but no one undertakes an excavation if by doing so he is going to undermine the habitations of the living so that they collapse and bury people under their ruins. The doctrines of religion are not a subject one can quibble about like any other. Our civilization is built up on them, and the maintenance of human society is based on the majority of men's believing in the truth of those doctrines. If men are taught that there is no almighty and all-just God, no divine world-order and no future life, they will feel exempt from all obligation to obey the precepts of civilization. Everyone will, without inhibition or fear, follow his asocial, egoistic instincts and seek to exercise his power; Chaos, which we have banished through many thousands of years of the work of civilization, will come again. Even if we knew, and could prove, that religion was not in possession of the truth, we ought to conceal the fact and behave in the way prescribed by the philosophy of "As if"—and this in the interest of the preservation of us all. And apart from the danger of the undertaking, it would be a purposeless cruelty. Countless people find their one consolation in religious doctrines, and can only bear life with their help. You would rob them of their support, without having anything better to give them in exchange. It is admitted that so far science has not achieved much, but even if it had advanced much further it would not suffice for man. Man has imperative needs of another sort, which can never be satisfied by cold science; and it is very strange—indeed, it is the height of inconsistency—that a psychologist who has always insisted on what a minor part is played in human affairs by the intelligence as compared with the life of the instincts—that such a psychologist should now try to rob mankind of a precious wish-fulfilment and should propose to compensate them for it with intellectual nourishment.'

What a lot of accusations all at once! Nevertheless I am ready with rebuttals for them all; and, what is more, I shall assert the view that civilization runs a greater risk if we maintain our present attitude to religion than if we give it up.

But I hardly know where to begin my reply. Perhaps with the assurance that I myself regard my undertaking as completely harmless and free of risk. It is not I who am overvaluing the intellect this time. If people are as my opponents describe them—and I should not like to contradict them—then there is no danger of a devout believer's being overcome by my arguments and deprived of his faith. Besides, I have said nothing which other and better men have not said before me in a much more complete, forcible and impressive manner. Their names are well known, and I shall not cite them, for I should not like to give an impression that I am seeking to rank myself as one of them. All I have done—and this is the only thing that is new in my exposition—is to add some psychological foundation to the criticisms of my great predecessors. It is hardly to be expected that precisely this addition will produce the effect which was denied to those earlier efforts. No doubt I might be asked here what is the point of writing these things if I am certain that they will be ineffective. But I shall come back to that later.

The one person this publication may injure is myself. I shall have to listen to the most disagreeable reproaches for my shallowness, narrow-mindedness and lack of idealism or of understanding for the highest interests of mankind. But on the one hand, such remonstrances are not new to me; and on the other, if a man has already learnt in his youth to rise superior to the disapproval of his contemporaries, what can it matter to him in his old age when he is certain soon to be beyond the reach of all favour or disfavour? In former times it was different. Then utterances such as mine brought with them a sure curtailment of one's earthly existence and an effective speeding-up of the opportunity for gaining a personal experience of the after-life. But, I repeat, those times are past and to-day writings such as this bring no more danger to their author than to their readers. The most that can happen is that the translation and distribution of his book will be forbidden in one country or another—and precisely, of course, in a country that is convinced of the high standard of its culture. But if one puts in any plea at all for the renunciation of wishes and for acquiescence in Fate, one must be able to tolerate this kind of injury too.

The further question occurred to me whether the publication of this work might not after all do harm. Not to a person, however, but to a cause—the cause of psycho-analysis. For it cannot be denied that psycho-analysis is my creation, and it has met with plenty of mistrust and ill-will. If I now come forward with such displeasing pronouncements, people will be only too ready to make a displacement from my person to psychoanalysis. 'Now we see,' they will say, 'where psycho-analysis leads to. The mask has fallen; it leads to a denial of God and of a moral ideal, as we always suspected. To keep us from this discovery we have been deluded into thinking that psycho-analysis has no *Weltanschauung* and never can construct one.'[1]

---

[1] [See some remarks at the end of Chapter II of *Inhibitions, Symptoms and Anxiety* (1926d), Standard Ed., **20**, 95–6; *I.P.L.*, **28**, 9–10.]

An outcry of this kind will really be disagree-able to me on account of my many fellow-workers, some of whom do not by any means share my attitude to the problems of religion. But psycho-analysis has already weathered many storms and now it must brave this fresh one. In point of fact psycho-analysis is a method of research, an im-partial instrument, like the infinitesimal calculus, as it were. If a physicist were to discover with the latter's help that after a certain time the earth would be destroyed, we would nevertheless hesi-tate to attribute destructive tendencies to the cal-culus itself and therefore to proscribe it. Nothing that I have said here against the truth-value of religions needed the support of psycho-analysis; it had been said by others long before analysis came into existence. If the application of the psycho-analytic method makes it possible to find a new argument against the truths of religion, *tant pis* for religion; but defenders of religion will by the same right make use of psycho-analysis in order to give full value to the affective signifi-cance of religious doctrines.

And now to proceed with our defence. Re-ligion has clearly performed great services for human civilization. It has contributed much to-wards the taming of the asocial instincts. But not enough. It has ruled human society for many thousands of years and has had time to show what it can achieve. If it had succeeded in making the majority of mankind happy, in comforting them, in reconciling them to life and in making them into vehicles of civilization, no one would dream of attempting to alter the existing conditions. But what do we see instead? We see that an appallingly large number of people are dissatisfied with civilization and unhappy in it, and feel it as a yoke which must be shaken off; and that these people either do everything in their power to change that civilization, or else go so far in their hostility to it that they will have nothing to do with civilization or with a restriction of instinct. At this point it will be objected against us that this state of affairs is due to the very fact that religion has lost a part of its influence over human masses precisely because of the deplorable effect of the advances of science. We will note this admission and the reason given for it, and we shall make use of it later for our own purposes; but the objection itself has no force.

It is doubtful whether men were in general happier at a time when religious doctrines held unrestricted sway; more moral they certainly were not. They have always known how to externalize the precepts of religion and thus to nullify their intentions. The priests, whose duty it was to ensure obedience to religion, met them half-way in this. God's kindness must lay a restraining hand on His justice. One sinned, and then one made a sacrifice or did penance and then one was free to sin once more. Russian introspectiveness has reached the pitch of concluding that sin is indispensable for the enjoyment of all the blessings of divine grace, so that, at bottom, sin is pleasing to God. It is no secret that the priests could only keep the masses submissive to religion by making such large concessions as these to the instinctual nature of man. Thus it was agreed: God alone is strong and good, man is weak and sinful. In every age immorality has found no less support in religion than morality has. If the achievements of religion in respect to man's happiness, susceptibility to culture[2] and moral control are no better than this, the question cannot but arise whether we are not overrating its necessity for mankind, and whether we do wisely in basing our cultural demands upon it.

Let us consider the unmistakable situation as it is to-day. We have heard the admission that religion no longer has the same influence on people that it used to. (We are here concerned with European Christian civilization.) And this is not because its promises have grown less but because people find them less credible. Let us admit that the reason—though perhaps not the only reason—for this change is the increase of the scientific spirit in the higher strata of human society. Criti-

[2] [The nature of 'susceptibility to culture' had been discussed by Freud in the first section of his paper on 'War and Death' (1915b), *Standard Ed.*, **14,** 283.]

cism has whittled away the evidential value of religious documents, natural science has shown up the errors in them, and comparative research has been struck by the fatal resemblance between the religious ideas which we revere and the mental products of primitive peoples and times.

The scientific spirit brings about a particular attitude towards worldly matters; before religious matters it pauses for a little, hesitates, and finally there too crosses the threshold. In this process there is no stopping; the greater the number of men to whom the treasures of knowledge become accessible, the more widespread is the falling-away from religious belief—at first only from its obsolete and objectionable trappings, but later from its fundamental postulates as well. The Americans who instituted the 'monkey trial' at Dayton[3] have alone shown themselves consistent. Elsewhere the inevitable transition is accomplished by way of half-measures and insincerities.

Civilization has little to fear from educated people and brain-workers. In them the replacement of religious motives for civilized behaviour by other, secular motives would proceed unobtrusively; moreover, such people are to a large extent themselves vehicles of civilization. But it is another matter with the great mass of the un-

[3] [A small town in Tennessee where, in 1925, a science teacher was prosecuted for breach of a State law by teaching that 'man is descended from the lower animals'.]

educated and oppressed, who have every reason for being enemies of civilization. So long as they do not discover that people no longer believe in God, all is well. But they will discover it, infallibly, even if this piece of writing of mine is not published. And they are ready to accept the results of scientific thinking, but without the change having taken place in them which scientific thinking brings about in people. Is there not a danger here that the hostility of these masses to civilization will throw itself against the weak spot that they have found in their task-mistress? If the sole reason why you must not kill your neighbour is because God has forbidden it and will severely punish you for it in this or the next life—then, when you learn that there is no God and that you need not fear His punishment, you will certainly kill your neighbour without hesitation, and you can only be prevented from doing so by mundane force. Thus either these dangerous masses must be held down most severely and kept most carefully away from any chance of intellectual awakening, or else the relationship between civilization and religion must undergo a fundamental revision.

VIII

ONE might think that there would be no special difficulties in the way of carrying out this latter proposal. It is true that it would involve a certain amount of renunciation, but more would perhaps be gained than lost, and a great danger would be avoided. Everyone is frightened of it, however, as though it would expose civilization to a still greater danger. When St. Boniface[1] cut down the tree that was venerated as sacred by the Saxons the bystanders expected some fearful event to follow upon the sacrilege. But nothing happened, and the Saxons accepted baptism.

When civilization laid down the commandment that a man shall not kill the neighbour whom he hates or who is in his way or whose property he covets, this was clearly done in the interest of man's communal existence, which would not otherwise be practicable. For the murderer would draw down on himself the vengeance of the murdered man's kinsmen and the secret envy of others, who within themselves feel as much inclined

[1] [The eighth-century, Devonshire-born, 'Apostle of Germany'.]

as he does for such acts of violence. Thus he would not enjoy his revenge or his robbery for long, but would have every prospect of soon being killed himself. Even if he protected himself against his single foes by extraordinary strength and caution, he would be bound to succumb to a combination of weaker men. If a combination of this sort did not take place, the murdering would continue endlessly and the final outcome would be that men would exterminate one another. We should arrive at the same state of affairs between individuals as still persists in Corsica between families, though elsewhere only between nations. Insecurity of life, which is an equal danger for everyone, now unites men into a society which prohibits the individual from killing and reserves to itself the right to communal killing of anyone who violates the prohibition. Here, then, we have justice and punishment.

But we do not publish this rational explanation of the prohibition against murder. We assert that the prohibition has been issued by God. Thus we take it upon ourselves to guess His intentions, and we find that He, too, is unwilling for men to exterminate one another. In behaving in this way we are investing the cultural prohibition with a quite special solemnity, but at the same time we risk making its observance dependent on belief in God. If we retrace this step—if we no longer attribute to God what is our own will and if we content ourselves with giving the social reason—then, it is true, we have renounced the transfiguration of the cultural prohibition, but we have also avoided the risk to it. But we gain something else as well. Through some kind of diffusion or infection, the character of sanctity and inviolability —of belonging to another world, one might say— has spread from a few major prohibitions on to every other cultural regulation, law and ordinance. But on these the halo often looks far from becoming: not only do they invalidate one another by giving contrary decisions at different times and places, but apart from this they show every sign of human inadequacy. It is easy to recognize in them things that can only be the product of short-sighted apprehensiveness or an expression of selfishly narrow interests or a conclusion based on insufficient premisses. The criticism which we cannot fail to level at them also diminishes to an unwelcome extent our respect for other, more justifiable cultural demands. Since it is an awkward task to separate what God Himself has demanded from what can be traced to the authority of an all-powerful parliament or a high judiciary, it would be an undoubted advantage if we were to leave God out altogether and honestly admit the purely human origin of all the regulations and precepts of civilization. Along with their pretended sanctity, these commandments and laws would lose their rigidity and unchangeableness as well. People could understand that they are made, not so much to rule them as, on the contrary, to serve their interests; and they would adopt a more friendly attitude to them, and instead of aiming at their abolition, would aim only at their improvement. This would be an important advance along the road which leads to becoming reconciled to the burden of civilization.

But here our plea for ascribing purely rational reasons to the precepts of civilization—that is to say, for deriving them from social necessity—is interrupted by a sudden doubt. We have chosen as our example the origin of the prohibition against murder. But does our account of it tally with historical truth? We fear not; it appears to be nothing but a rationalistic construction. With the help of psycho-analysis, we have made a study of precisely this piece of the cultural history of mankind,[2] and, basing ourselves on it, we are bound to say that in reality things happened otherwise. Even in present-day man purely reasonable motives can effect little against passionate impulses. How much weaker then must they have been in the human animal of primaeval times! Perhaps his descendants would even now kill one another without inhibition, if it were not that among those murderous acts there was one— the killing of the primitive father—which evoked an irresistible emotional reaction with momen-

[2] [Cf. the fourth essay in *Totem and Taboo* (1912–13).]

tous consequences. From it arose the commandment: Thou shalt not kill. Under totemism this commandment was restricted to the father-substitute; but it was later extended to other people, though even to-day it is not universally obeyed.

But, as was shown by arguments which I need not repeat here, the primal father was the original image of God, the model on which later generations have shaped the figure of God. Hence the religious explanation is right. God actually played a part in the genesis of that prohibition; it was His influence, not any insight into social necessity, which created it. And the displacement of man's will on to God is fully justified. For men knew that they had disposed of their father by violence, and in their reaction to that impious deed, they determined to respect his will thenceforward. Thus religious doctrine tells us the historical truth —though subject, it is true, to some modification and disguise—whereas our rational account disavows it.

We now observe that the store of religious ideas includes not only wish-fulfilments but important historical recollections. This concurrent influence of past and present must give religion a truly incomparable wealth of power. But perhaps with the help of an analogy yet another discovery may begin to dawn on us. Though it is not a good plan to transplant ideas far from the soil in which they grew up, yet here is a conformity which we cannot avoid pointing out. We know that a human child cannot successfully complete its development to the civilized stage without passing through a phase of neurosis sometimes of greater and sometimes of less distinctness. This is because so many instinctual demands which will later be unserviceable cannot be suppressed by the rational operation of the child's intellect but have to be tamed by acts of repression, behind which, as a rule, lies the motive of anxiety. Most of these infantile neuroses are overcome spontaneously in the course of growing up, and this is especially true of the obsessional neuroses of childhood. The remainder can be cleared up later still by psycho-analytic treatment. In just the same way, one might assume, humanity as a whole, in its development through the ages, fell into states analogous to the neuroses,[3] and for the same reasons—namely because in the times of its ignorance and intellectual weakness the instinctual renunciations indispensable for man's communal existence had only been achieved by it by means of purely affective forces. The precipitates of these processes resembling repression which took place in prehistoric times still remained attached to civilization for long periods. Religion

[3] [Freud returned to this question at the end of his *Civilization and Its Discontents* (1930a), S.E., **21**, 144, in the last of the *New Introductory Lectures* (1933a) and in Chapter III of *Moses and Monotheism* (1939a).]

would thus be the universal obsessional neurosis of humanity; like the obsessional neurosis of children, it arose out of the Oedipus complex, out of the relation to the father. If this view is right, it is to be supposed that a turning-away from religion is bound to occur with the fatal inevitability of a process of growth, and that we find ourselves at this very juncture in the middle of that phase of development. Our behaviour should therefore be modelled on that of a sensible teacher who does not oppose an impending new development but seeks to ease its path and mitigate the violence of its irruption. Our analogy does not, to be sure, exhaust the essential nature of religion. If, on the one hand, religion brings with it obsessional restrictions, exactly as an individual obsessional neurosis does, on the other hand it comprises a system of wishful illusions together with a disavowal[4] of reality, such as we find in an isolated form nowhere else but in amentia,[5] in a state of blissful hallucinatory confusion. But these are only analogies, by the help of which we endeavour to understand a social phenomenon; the pathology of the individual does not supply us with a fully valid counterpart.

It has been repeatedly pointed out (by myself

---

4 [See the paper on 'Fetishism' (1927e), S.E., **21**, 153.]

5 ['Meynert's amentia': a state of acute hallucinatory confusion.]

and in particular by Theodor Reik[6]) in how great detail the analogy between religion and obsessional neurosis can be followed out, and how many of the peculiarities and vicissitudes in the formation of religion can be understood in that light. And it tallies well with this that devout believers are safeguarded in a high degree against the risk of certain neurotic illnesses; their acceptance of the universal neurosis spares them the task of constructing a personal one.[7]

Our knowledge of the historical worth of certain religious doctrines increases our respect for them, but does not invalidate our proposal that they should cease to be put forward as the reasons for the precepts of civilization. On the contrary! Those historical residues have helped us to view religious teachings, as it were, as neurotic relics, and we may now argue that the time has probably come, as it does in an analytic treatment, for replacing the effects of repression by the results of the rational operation of the intellect. We may foresee, but hardly regret, that such a process of remoulding will not stop at renouncing the solemn transfiguration of cultural precepts, but that a general revision of them will result in many of

[6] [Cf. Freud, 'Obsessive Actions and Religious Practices' (1907b) and Reik (1927).]

[7] [Freud had often made this point before: e.g. in a sentence added in 1919 to his study on Leonardo da Vinci (1910c), Standard Ed., 11, 123.]

them being done away with. In this way our appointed task of reconciling men to civilization will to a great extent be achieved. We need not deplore the renunciation of historical truth when we put forward rational grounds for the precepts of civilization. The truths contained in religious doctrines are after all so distorted and systematically disguised that the mass of humanity cannot recognize them as truth. The case is similar to what happens when we tell a child that new-born babies are brought by the stork. Here, too, we are telling the truth in symbolic clothing, for we know what the large bird signifies. But the child does not know it. He hears only the distorted part of what we say, and feels that he has been deceived; and we know how often his distrust of the grown-ups and his refractoriness actually take their start from this impression. We have become convinced that it is better to avoid such symbolic disguisings of the truth in what we tell children and not to withhold from them a knowledge of the true state of affairs commensurate with their intellectual level.[8]

[8] [Freud later drew a distinction between what he termed 'material' and 'historical' truth in several passages. See, in particular, Section G of Part II of Chapter III of *Moses and Monotheism* (1939a). Cf. also an Editor's footnote on the subject in Chapter XII (C) of *The Psychopathology of Everyday Life* (1901b), *Standard Ed.*, **6**, 256.]

IX

'You permit yourself contradictions which are hard to reconcile with one another. You begin by saying that a piece of writing like yours is quite harmless: no one will let himself be robbed of his faith by considerations of the sort put forward in it. But since it is nevertheless your intention, as becomes evident later on, to upset that faith, we may ask why in fact you are publishing your work? In another passage, moreover, you admit that it may be dangerous, indeed very dangerous, for someone to discover that people no longer believe in God. Hitherto he has been docile, but now he throws off his obedience to the precepts of civilization. Yet your whole contention that basing the commandments of civilization on religious grounds constitutes a danger for civilization rests on the assumption that the believer can be turned into an unbeliever. Surely that is a complete contradiction.

'And here is another. On the one hand you admit that men cannot be guided through their intelligence, they are ruled by their passions and their instinctual demands. But on the other hand you propose to replace the affective basis of their obedience to civilization by a rational one. Let who can understand this. To me it seems that it must be either one thing or the other.

'Besides, have you learned nothing from history? Once before an attempt of this kind was made to substitute reason for religion, officially and in the grand manner. Surely you remember the French Revolution and Robespierre? And you must also remember how short-lived and miserably ineffectual the experiment was? The same experiment is being repeated in Russia at the present time, and we need not feel curious as to its outcome. Do you not think we may take it for granted that men cannot do without religion?

'You have said yourself that religion is more than an obsessional neurosis. But you have not dealt with this other side of it. You are content to work out the analogy with a neurosis. Men, you say, must be freed from a neurosis. What else may be lost in the process is of no concern to you.'

The appearance of contradiction has probably come about because I have dealt with complicated matters too hurriedly. But we can remedy this to some extent. I still maintain that what I have written is quite harmless in one respect. No believer will let himself be led astray from his faith by these or any similar arguments. A believer is bound to the teachings of religion by certain ties of affection. But there are undoubtedly countless other people who are not in the same sense believers. They obey the precepts of civilization because they let themselves be intimidated by the threats of religion, and they are afraid of religion so long as they have to consider it as a part of the reality which hems them in. They are the people who break away as soon as they are allowed to give up their belief in the reality-value of religion. But they too are unaffected by arguments. They cease to fear religion when they observe that others do not fear it; and it was of them that I asserted that they would get to know about the decline of religious influence even if I did not publish my work. [Cf. p. 64.]

But I think you yourself attach more weight to the other contradiction which you charge me with. Since men are so little accessible to reasonable arguments and are so entirely governed by their instinctual wishes, why should one set out to deprive them of an instinctual satisfaction and replace it by reasonable arguments? It is true that men are like this; but have you asked yourself whether they *must* be like this, whether their innermost nature necessitates it? Can an anthropologist give the cranial index of a people whose custom it is to deform their children's heads by bandaging them round from their earliest years? Think of the depressing contrast between the radiant intelligence of a healthy child and the feeble intellectual powers of the average adult. Can we be quite certain that it is not precisely religious education which bears a large share of the blame for this relative atrophy? I think it would be a very long time before a child who was not influenced began to trouble himself about God and things in another world. Perhaps his thoughts on these matters would then take the same paths as they did with his forefathers. But we do not wait for such a development; we introduce him to the doctrines of religion at an age when he is neither interested in them nor capable of grasping their import. Is it not true that the two main points in the programme for the education of children today are retardation of sexual development and premature religious influence? Thus by the time the child's intellect awakens, the doctrines of religion have already become unassailable. But are you of opinion that it is very conducive to the strengthening of the intellectual function that so important a field should be closed against it by the threat of Hell-fire? When a man has once brought himself to accept uncritically all the absurdities that religious doctrines put before him and even to overlook the contradictions between them, we need not be greatly surprised at the weakness of his intellect. But we have no other means of controlling our instinctual nature but our intelligence. How can we expect people who are under the dominance of prohibitions of thought to attain the psychological ideal, the primacy of the intelligence? You know, too, that women in general are said to suffer from 'physiological feeble-mindedness'[1]—that is, from a lesser intelligence than men. The fact itself is disputable and its interpretation doubtful, but one argument in favour of this intellectual atrophy being of a secondary nature is that women labour under the harshness of an early prohibition against turning their thoughts to what would most have interested them—namely, the problems of sexual life. So long as a person's early years are influenced not only by a sexual inhibition of thought but also by a religious inhibition and by a loyal inhibition[2] derived from this, we cannot really tell what in fact he is like.

But I will moderate my zeal and admit the possibility that I, too, am chasing an illusion. Perhaps the effect of the religious prohibition of thought may not be so bad as I suppose; perhaps it will turn out that human nature remains the same even if education is not abused in order to subject people to religion. I do not know and you cannot know either. It is not only the great problems of this life that seem insoluble at the

1 [The phrase was used by Moebius (1903). Cf. Freud's early paper on 'civilized' sexual morality (1908d), *Standard Ed.*, 9, 199, where the present argument is anticipated.]

2 [I.e. in regard to the Monarchy.]

present time; many lesser questions too are difficult to answer. But you must admit that here we are justified in having a hope for the future—that perhaps there is a treasure to be dug up capable of enriching civilization and that it is worth making the experiment of an irreligious education. Should the experiment prove unsatisfactory I am ready to give up the reform and to return to my earlier, purely descriptive judgement that man is a creature of weak intelligence who is ruled by his instinctual wishes.

On another point I agree with you unreservedly. It is certainly senseless to begin by trying to do away with religion by force and at a single blow. Above all, because it would be hopeless. The believer will not let his belief be torn from him, either by arguments or by prohibitions. And even if this did succeed with some it would be cruelty. A man who has been taking sleeping draughts for tens of years is naturally unable to sleep if his sleeping draught is taken away from him. That the effect of religious consolations may be likened to that of a narcotic is well illustrated by what is happening in America. There they are now trying—obviously under the influence of petticoat government—to deprive people of all stimulants, intoxicants, and other pleasure-producing substances, and instead, by way of compensation, are surfeiting them with piety. This is another experiment as to whose outcome we need not feel curious [p. 76].[3]

Thus I must contradict you when you go on to argue that men are completely unable to do without the consolation of the religious illusion, that without it they could not bear the troubles of life and the cruelties of reality. That is true, certainly, of the men into whom you have instilled the sweet—or bitter-sweet—poison from childhood onwards. But what of the other men, who have been sensibly brought up? Perhaps those who do not suffer from the neurosis will need no intoxicant to deaden it. They will, it is true, find themselves in a difficult situation. They will have to admit to themselves the full extent of their helplessness and their insignificance in the machinery of the universe; they can no longer be the centre of creation, no longer the object of tender care on the part of a beneficent Providence. They will be in the same position as a child who has left the parental house where he was so warm and comfortable. But surely infantilism is destined to be surmounted. Men cannot remain children for ever; they must in the end go out into 'hostile life'. We may call this *'education to reality'*. Need I confess to you that the sole purpose of my book is to point out the necessity for this forward step?

You are afraid, probably, that they will not

[3] [This was written in the middle of the period of National Prohibition in the United States (1920–33).]

stand up to the hard test? Well, let us at least hope they will. It is something, at any rate, to know that one is thrown upon one's own resources. One learns then to make a proper use of them. And men are not entirely without assistance. Their scientific knowledge has taught them much since the days of the Deluge, and it will increase their power still further. And, as for the great necessities of Fate, against which there is no help, they will learn to endure them with resignation. Of what use to them is the mirage of wide acres in the moon, whose harvest no one has ever yet seen? As honest smallholders on this earth they will know how to cultivate their plot in such a way that it supports them. By withdrawing their expectations from the other world and concentrating all their liberated energies into their life on earth, they will probably succeed in achieving a state of things in which life will become tolerable for everyone and civilization no longer oppressive to anyone. Then, with one of our fellow-unbelievers, they will be able to say without regret:

> *Den Himmel überlassen wir*
> *Den Engeln und den Spatzen.*[4]

[4] ['We leave Heaven to the angels and the sparrows.' From Heine's poem *Deutschland* (Caput I). The word which is here translated 'fellow-unbelievers'—in German *'Unglaubensgenossen'*—was applied by Heine himself to Spinoza. It had been quoted by Freud as an example of a particular kind of joke-technique in his book on jokes (1905c), *Standard Ed.*, **8**, 77.]

X

'THAT sounds splendid! A race of men who have renounced all illusions and have thus become capable of making their existence on earth tolerable! I, however, cannot share your expectations. And that is not because I am the obstinate reactionary you perhaps take me for. No, it is because I am sensible. We seem now to have exchanged roles: you emerge as an enthusiast who allows himself to be carried away by illusions, and I stand for the claims of reason, the rights of scepticism. What you have been expounding seems to me to be built upon errors which, following your example, I may call illusions, because they betray clearly enough the influence of your wishes. You pin your hope on the possibility that generations which have not experienced the influence of religious doctrines in early childhood will easily attain the desired primacy of the intelligence over the life of the instincts. This is surely an illusion: in this decisive respect human nature is hardly likely to change. If I am not mistaken—one knows so little about other civilizations—there are even to-day peoples which do not grow up under the pressure of a religious system, and yet they approach no nearer to your ideal than the rest. If you want to expel religion from our European civilization, you can only do it by means of another system of doctrines; and such a system would from the outset take over all the psychological characteristics of religion—the same sanctity, rigidity and intolerance, the same prohibition of thought—for its own defence. You have to have something of the kind in order to meet the requirements of education. And you cannot do without education. The path from the infant at the breast to the civilized man is a long one; too many human young would go astray on it and fail to reach their life-tasks at the proper time if they were left without guidance to their own development. The doctrines which had been applied in their upbringing would always set limits to the thinking of their riper years—which is exactly what you reproach religion with doing today. Do you not observe that it is an ineradicable and innate defect of our and every other civilization, that it imposes on children, who are driven by instinct and weak in intellect, the making of decisions which only the mature intelligence of adults can vindicate? But civilization cannot do otherwise, because of the fact that mankind's age-long development is compressed into a few years of childhood; and it is only by emotional forces that the child can be induced to master the task set before it. Such, then, are the prospects for your "primacy of the intellect".

'And now you must not be surprised if I plead on behalf of retaining the religious doctrinal system as the basis of education and of man's communal life. This is a practical problem, not a question of reality-value. Since, for the sake of preserving our civilization, we cannot postpone influencing the individual until he has become ripe for civilization (and many would never become so in any case), since we are obliged to impose on the growing child some doctrinal system which shall operate in him as an axiom that admits of no criticism, it seems to me that the religious system is by far the most suitable for the purpose. And it is so, of course, precisely on account of its wish-fulfilling and consolatory power, by which you claim to recognize it as an "illusion". In view of the difficulty of discovering anything about reality—indeed, of the doubt whether it is possible for us to do so at all—we must not overlook the fact that human needs, too, are a piece of reality, and, in fact, an important piece and one that concerns us especially closely.

'Another advantage of religious doctrine resides, to my mind, in one of its characteristics to which you seem to take particular exception. For it allows of a refinement and sublimation of ideas, which make it possible for it to be divested of most of the traces which it bears of primitive and infantile thinking. What then remains is a body of ideas which science no longer contradicts and is unable to disprove. These modifications of religious doctrine, which you have condemned as half-measures and compromises, make it possible to avoid the cleft between the uneducated masses and the philosophic thinker, and to preserve the common bond between them which is so important for the safeguarding of civilization. With this, there would be no need to fear that the men of the people would discover that the upper strata of society "no longer believe in God". I think I have now shown that your endeavours come down to an attempt to replace a proved and emotionally valuable illusion by another one, which is unproved and without emotional value.'

You will not find me inaccessible to your criticism. I know how difficult it is to avoid illusions; perhaps the hopes I have confessed to are of an illusory nature, too. But I hold fast to one distinction. Apart from the fact that no penalty is imposed for not sharing them, my illusions are not, like religious ones, incapable of correction. They have not the character of a delusion. If experience should show—not to me, but to others after me, who think as I do—that we have been mistaken, we will give up our expectations. Take my attempt for what it is. A psychologist who does not deceive himself about the difficulty of finding one's bearings in this world, makes an endeavour to assess the development of man, in the light of the small portion of knowledge he has gained through a study of the mental processes of individuals during their development from child to adult. In so doing, the idea forces itself upon him that religion is comparable to a childhood neurosis, and he is optimistic enough to suppose that mankind will surmount this neurotic phase, just as so many children grow out of their similar neurosis. These discoveries derived from individual psychology may be insufficient, their application to the human race unjustified, and his optimism unfounded. I grant you all these uncertainties. But often one cannot refrain from saying what one thinks, and one excuses oneself on the ground that one is not giving it out for more than it is worth.

And there are two points that I must dwell on a little longer. Firstly, the weakness of my position does not imply any strengthening of yours. I think you are defending a lost cause. We may insist as often as we like that man's intellect is powerless in comparison with his instinctual life, and we may be right in this. Nevertheless, there is something peculiar about this weakness. The voice of the intellect is a soft one, but it does not rest till it has gained a hearing. Finally, after a countless succession of rebuffs, it succeeds. This is one of the few points on which one may be optimistic about the future of mankind, but it is in itself a

point of no small importance. And from it one
can derive yet other hopes. The primacy of
the intellect lies, it is true, in a distant, distant
future, but probably not in an *infinitely* distant
one. It will presumably set itself the same aims as
those whose realization you expect from your God
(of course within human limits—so far as external
reality, 'Ανάκη, allows it), namely the love of
man and the decrease of suffering. This being so,
we may tell ourselves that our antagonism is only
a temporary one and not irreconcilable. We de-
sire the same things, but you are more impatient,
more exacting, and—why should I not say it?—
more self-seeking than I and those on my side.
You would have the state of bliss begin directly
after death; you expect the impossible from it and
you will not surrender the claims of the individual. Our God, Λόγος,[1] will fulfil whichever of
these wishes nature outside us allows, but he will
do it very gradually, only in the unforeseeable
future, and for a new generation of men. He
promises no compensation for us, who suffer
grievously from life. On the way to this distant
goal your religious doctrines will have to be dis-
carded, no matter whether the first attempts fail,
or whether the first substitutes prove to be untena-

---

[1] The twin gods Λόγος [*Logos:* Reason] and 'Ανάγκη
[*Ananke:* Necessity] of the Dutch writer Multatuli. [Cf.
an Editor's footnote to 'The Economic Problem of
Masochism' (1924c), *Standard Ed., 19,* 168.]

ble. You know why: in the long run nothing can withstand reason and experience, and the contradiction which religion offers to both is all too palpable. Even purified religious ideas cannot escape this fate, so long as they try to preserve anything of the consolation of religion. No doubt if they confine themselves to a belief in a higher spiritual being, whose qualities are indefinable and whose purposes cannot be discerned, they will be proof against the challenge of science; but then they will also lose their hold on human interest.

And secondly: observe the difference between your attitude to illusions and mine. You have to defend the religious illusion with all your might. If it becomes discredited—and indeed the threat to it is great enough—then your world collapses. There is nothing left for you but to despair of everything, of civilization and the future of mankind. From that bondage I am, we are, free. Since we are prepared to renounce a good part of our infantile wishes, we can bear it if a few of our expectations turn out to be illusions.

Education freed from the burden of religious doctrines will not, it may be, effect much change in men's psychological nature. Our god Λόγος is perhaps not a very almighty one, and he may only be able to fulfil a small part of what his predecessors have promised. If we have to acknowledge this we shall accept it with resignation. We shall not on that account lose our interest in the world and in life, for we have one sure support which you lack. We believe that it is possible for scientific work to gain some knowledge about the reality of the world, by means of which we can increase our power and in accordance with which we can arrange our life. If this belief is an illusion, then we are in the same position as you. But science has given us evidence by its numerous and important successes that it is no illusion. Science has many open enemies, and many more secret ones, among those who cannot forgive her for having weakened religious faith and for threatening to overthrow it. She is reproached for the smallness of the amount she has taught us and for the incomparably greater field she has left in obscurity. But, in this, people forget how young she is, how difficult her beginnings were and how infinitesimally small is the period of time since the human intellect has been strong enough for the tasks she sets. Are we not all at fault, in basing our judgements on periods of time that are too short? We should make the geologists our pattern. People complain of the unreliability of science—how she announces as a law to-day what the next generation recognizes as an error and replaces by a new law whose accepted validity lasts no longer. But this is unjust and in part untrue. The transformations of scientific opinion are developments, advances, not revolutions. A law which was held at first to be universally valid proves to be a special case of a more comprehensive uniformity, or is limited by another law, not discovered till later; a rough approximation to the truth is replaced by a more carefully adapted one, which in turn awaits further perfectioning. There are various fields where we have not yet surmounted a phase of research in which we make trial with hypotheses that soon have to be rejected as inadequate; but in other fields we already possess an assured and almost unalterable core of knowledge. Finally, an attempt has been made to discredit scientific endeavour in a radical way, on the ground that, being bound to the conditions of our own organization, it can yield nothing else than subjective results, whilst the real nature of things outside ourselves remains inaccessible. But this is to disregard several factors which are of decisive importance for the understanding of scientific work. In the first place, our organization—that is, our mental apparatus—has been developed precisely in the attempt to explore the external world, and it must therefore have realized in its structure some degree of expediency; in the second place, it is itself a constituent part of the world which we set out to investigate, and it readily admits of such an investigation; thirdly, the task of science is fully covered if we limit it to showing how the world must appear to us in consequence of the particular character of our organization; fourthly, the ultimate findings of science, precisely because of the way in which they are acquired, are determined not only by our organization but by the things which have affected that organization; finally, the problem of the nature of the world without regard to our percipient mental apparatus is an empty abstraction, devoid of practical interest.

No, our science is no illusion. But an illusion it would be to suppose that what science cannot give us we can get elsewhere.

LIST OF ABBREVIATIONS

G.S.	= Freud, *Gesammelte Schriften* (12 vols.), Vienna, 1924–34.
G.W.	= Freud, *Gesammelte Werke* (18 vols.), London, from 1940.
C.P.	= Freud, *Collected Papers* (5 vols.), London, 1924–50.
S.E. *Standard Ed.* }	= Freud, *Standard Edition* (24 vols.), London, from 1953.
I.P.L.	= *International Psycho-Analytical Library,* Hogarth Press and Institute of Psycho-Analysis, London, from 1921.

BIBLIOGRAPHY AND AUTHOR INDEX

[Titles of books and periodicals are in italics; titles of papers are in inverted commas. Abbreviations are in accordance with the *World List of Scientific Periodicals* (London, 1952). Further abbreviations used in this volume will be found in the List on page 93. Numerals in thick type refer to volumes; ordinary numerals refer to pages. The figures in round brackets at the end of each entry indicate the page or pages of this volume on which the work in question is mentioned. In the case of the Freud entries, the letters attached to the dates of publication are in accordance with the corresponding entries in the complete bibliography of Freud's writings to be included in the last volume of the *Standard Edition*.

For non-technical authors, and for technical authors where no specific work is mentioned, see the General Index.]

FREUD, S. (1899*a*) 'Über Deckerinnerungen', *G.S.*, **1**, 465; *G.W.*, **1**, 529. (29)
   [*Trans.*: 'Screen Memories', *C.P.*, **5**, 47; *Standard Ed.*, **3**, 301.]
   (1900*a*) *Die Traumdeutung*, Vienna. *G.S.*, **2–3**; *G.W.*, **2–3**. (23)
   [*Trans.*: *The Interpretation of Dreams*, London and New York, 1955; *Standard Ed.*, **4–5**.]

(1901*b*) *Zur Psychopathologie des Alltagslebens*, Berlin, 1904. *G.S.*, **4**, 3; *G.W.*, **4**. (73)
[*Trans.:* The Psychopathology of Everyday Life, Standard Ed., **6.**]

(1905*c*) *Der Witz und seine Beziehung zum Unbewussten*, Vienna. *G.S.*, **9**, 5; *G.W.*, **6**. (82)
[*Trans.:* Jokes and their Relation to the Unconscious, London, 1960; Standard Ed., **8.**]

(1907*b*) 'Zwangshandlungen und Religionsübung', *G.S.*, **10**, 210; *G.W.*, **7**, 129. (x, 71–72)
[*Trans.:* 'Obsessive Actions and Religious Practices', *C.P.*, **2**, 25; Standard Ed., **9**, 116.]

(1908*d*) 'Die "kulturelle" Sexualmoral und die moderne Nervosität', *G.S.*, **5**, 143; *G.W.*, **7**, 143. (79)
[*Trans.:* ' "Civilized" Sexual Morality and Modern Nervous Illness', *C.P.*, **2**, 76; Standard Ed., **9**, 179.]

(1908*e* [1907]) 'Der Dichter und das Phantasieren', *G.S.*, **10**, 229; *G.W.*, **7**, 213. (18)
[*Trans.:* 'Creative Writers and Day-Dreaming', *C.P.*, **4**, 173; Standard Ed., **9**, 143.]

(1910*c*) *Eine Kindheitserinnerung des Leonardo da Vinci*, Vienna. *G.S.*, **9**, 371; *G.W.*, **8**, 128. (72)
[*Trans.:* Leonardo da Vinci and a Memory of his Childhood, Standard Ed., **11**, 59.]

(1912–13) *Totem und Tabu*, Vienna, 1913. *G.S.*, **10**, 3; *G.W.*, **9**. (x, 24, 32–35, 68)
[*Trans.:* Totem and Taboo, London, 1950; New York, 1952; Standard Ed., **13**, 3.]

(1914*c*) 'Zur Einführung des Narzissmus', *G.S.*, **6**, 155; *G.W.*, **10**, 138. (34)

[*Trans.:* 'On Narcissism: an Introduction', *C.P.*, **4**, 30; *Standard Ed.*, **14**, 69.]

(1915*b*) 'Zeitgemässes über Krieg und Tod', *G.S.*, **10**, 315; *G.W.*, **10**, 324. (62)

[*Trans.:* 'Thoughts for the Times on War and Death', *C.P.*, **4**, 288; *Standard Ed.*, **14**, 275.]

(1921*c*) *Massenpsychologie und Ich-Analyse*, Vienna. *G.S.*, **6**, 261; *G.W.*, **13**, 73. (5)

[*Trans.:* *Group Psychology and the Analysis of the Ego*, *Standard Ed.*, **18**, 67; *I.P.L.*, **6**.]

(1923*b*) *Das Ich und das Es*, Vienna. *G.S.*, **6**, 353; *G.W.*, **13**, 237. (13)

[*Trans.:* *The Ego and the Id*, *Standard Ed.*, **19**, 3; *I.P.L.*, **12**.]

(1924*c*) 'Das ökonomische Problem des Masochismus', *G.S.*, **5**, 374; *G.W.*, **13**, 371. (88)

[*Trans.:* 'The Economic Problem of Masochism', *C.P.*, **2**, 255; *Standard Ed.*, **19**, 157.]

(1926*d*) *Hemmung, Symptom und Angst*, Vienna. *G.S.*, **11**, 23; *G.W.*, **14**, 113. (59)

[*Trans.:* *Inhibitions, Symptoms and Anxiety*, *Standard Ed.*, **20**, 77; *I.P.L.*, **28**.]

(1926*e*) *Die Frage der Laienanalyse*, Vienna. *G.S.*, **11**, 307; *G.W.*, **14**, 209. (29)

[*Trans.:* *The Question of Lay Analysis*, London, 1947; *Standard Ed.*, **20**, 179.]

(1927*c*) *Die Zukunft einer Illusion*, Vienna. *G.S.*, **11**, 411; *G.W.*, **14**, 325.

[*Trans.:* *The Future of an Illusion*, New York, 1928; *Standard Ed.*, **21**, 3; *I.P.L.*, **15**.]

(1927*e*) 'Fetischismus', *G.S.*, **11**, 395; *G.W.*, **14**, 311. (71)

[*Trans.:* 'Fetishism', *C.P.*, **5**, 198; *Standard Ed.*, **21**, 149.]

(1930a) *Das Unbehagen in der Kultur*, Vienna. *G.S.*, **12**, 29; *G.W.*, **14**, 421. (x, 3, 8, 70)
[*Trans.: Civilization and Its Discontents*, London, 1930; New York, 1961; *Standard Ed.*, **21**, 59.]

(1933a) *Neue Folge der Vorlesungen zur Einführung in die Psychoanalyse*, Vienna. *G.S.*, **12**, 151; *G.W.*, **15**, 207. (x, 8, 70)
[*Trans.: New Introductory Lectures on Psycho-Analysis*, London and New York, 1933; *Standard Ed.*, **22**.]

(1933b) *Warum Krieg?*, *G.S.*, **12**, 349; *G.W.*, **16**, 13. (x, 8)
[*Trans.: Why War? C.P.*, **5**, 273; *Standard Ed.*, **22**.]

(1935a) Postscript (1935) to *An Autobiographical Study*, new edition, London and New York; *Standard Ed.*, **20**, 71. (ix)
[*German Text:* 'Nachschrift 1935 zur *Selbstdarstellung*', 2nd edition, Vienna, 1936; *G.W.*, **16**, 31. German original first appeared late in 1935.]

(1936a) Letter to Romain Rolland: 'Eine Erinnerungsstörung auf der Akropolis', *G.W.*, **16**, 250. (38)
[*Trans.:* 'A Disturbance of Memory on the Acropolis', *C.P.*, **5**, 302; *Standard Ed.*, **22**.]

(1939a [1937–9]) *Der Mann Moses und die monotheistische Religion*, *G.W.*, **16**, 103. (x, 70, 73)
[*Trans.: Moses and Monotheism*, London and New York, 1939; *Standard Ed.*, **23**.]

MOEBIUS, P. J. (1903) *Über den physiologischen Schwachsinn des Weibes* (5th ed.), Halle. (79)

REIK, T. (1927) 'Dogma und Zwangsidee: eine psychoanalytische Studie zur Entwicklung der Religion', *Imago,* **13,** 247; in book form, Vienna, 1927. (71–72)
[*Trans.:* In *Dogma and Compulsions: Psychoanalytic Studies on Myths and Religions,* New York, 1951.]

VAIHINGER, H. (1922) *Die Philosophie des Als Ob,* Berlin. (7th and 8th ed.; 1st ed., 1911.) (43–45)
[*Trans.: The Philosophy of 'As if',* London, 1924.]

GENERAL INDEX

This index includes the names of non-technical authors. It also includes the names of technical authors where no reference is made in the text to specific works. For reference to specific technical works, the Bibliography should be consulted.

ANCHOR BOOKS

PSYCHOLOGY

ALLPORT, GORDON W.   The Nature of Prejudice, A149

BETTELHEIM, BRUNO   Paul and Mary: Two Case Histories from *Truants from Life,* A237

BRENNER, CHARLES   An Elementary Textbook of Psychoanalysis, A102

FREUD, SIGMUND   The Future of an Illusion, A99

—— A General Selection from the Works of Sigmund Freud, ed. Rickman, A115

FROMM, ERICH   May Man Prevail?, A275

GOFFMAN, ERVING   Asylums: Essays on the Social Situation of Mental Patients and Other Inmates, A277

—— The Presentation of Self in Everyday Life, A174

JONES, ERNEST   Hamlet and Oedipus, A31

—— The Life and Work of Sigmund Freud, ed. & abr. in 1 vol. Trilling & Marcus, A340

JUNG, C. G.   Psyche and Symbol, A136

RIEFF, PHILIP   Freud: The Mind of the Moralist, A278

VICO, GIAMBATTISTA   The New Science of Giambattista Vico, trans. Bergin & Fisch, A254

WHYTE, LANCELOT LAW   The Unconscious Before Freud, A286

WIENER, NORBERT   The Human Use of Human Beings, A34

ANCHOR BOOKS

PHILOSOPHY AND RELIGION

ALBRIGHT, WILLIAM FOXWELL From the Stone Age to Christianity, A100

ARENDT, HANNAH The Human Condition, A182

BARRETT, WILLIAM Irrational Man, A321

BARTH, KARL Community, State and Church, A221

BENZ, ERNST The Eastern Orthodox Church—Its Thought and Life, trans. Winston, A332

BERENSON, BERNARD Aesthetics and History, A36

BERGSON, HENRI *Laughter* (with Meredith's *Essay on Comedy*) in Comedy, A87

—— Matter and Memory, A172

—— The Two Sources of Morality and Religion, A28

BROWN, ROBERT MCAFEE, & WEIGEL, GUSTAVE, S.J. An American Dialogue, A257

BURKE, EDMUND Edmund Burke: Selected Writings and Speeches, ed. Stanlis, A334

BURTT, E. A. The Metaphysical Foundations of Modern Science, A41

CARY, JOYCE Art and Reality, A260

CROSS, FRANK MOORE, JR. The Ancient Library of Qumran, A272

FORSTER, E. M. Alexandria: A History and a Guide, A231

FREUD, SIGMUND The Future of an Illusion, A99

GALILEO Discoveries and Opinions of Galileo, trans. Drake, A94

GASTER, THEODOR H. The Dead Sea Scriptures, A92

HEIDEGGER, MARTIN An Introduction to Metaphysics, A251

HERBERG, WILL, ed. Four Existentialist Theologians, A141

—— Protestant-Catholic-Jew, A195

JASPERS, KARL Man in the Modern Age, A101

KAUFMANN, WALTER Critique of Religion and Philosophy, A252

—— The Faith of a Heretic, A336

—— From Shakespeare to Existentialism, A213

KIERKEGAARD, S. Either/Or: 2 vols., A181a, A181b

—— Fear and Trembling *and* The Sickness unto Death, A30

KRAMER, SAMUEL NOAH, ed. Mythologies of the Ancient World, A229

LEITH, JOHN H., ed. Creeds of the Churches: A Reader in Christian Doctrine from the Bible to the Present, A312

LENSKI, GERHARD The Religious Factor, A337

LITTELL, FRANKLIN H. From State Church to Pluralism, A294

LOWRIE, WALTER A Short Life of Kierkegaard, A273

LUTHER, MARTIN Martin Luther: Selections from His Writings, ed. Dillenberger, A271

MARX, KARL, & ENGELS, FRIEDRICH Basic Writings on Politics and Philosophy, A185

MEREDITH, GEORGE Essay on Comedy (with Bergson's *Laughter*) in Comedy, A87

MEYERHOFF, HANS, ed. The Philosophy of History in Our Time, A164

MURRAY, GILBERT Five Stages of Greek Religion, A51

NEWMAN, JAMES R. Science and Sensibility, A357

NIETZSCHE, FRIEDRICH The Birth of Tragedy and The Genealogy of Morals, A81

ORTEGA Y GASSET, JOSE The Dehumanization of Art and Other Writings on Art and Culture, A72

PAOLUCCI, HENRY & ANNE, eds. Hegel on Tragedy, A276

PEIRCE, CHARLES S. Values in a Universe of Chance, A126

RATHMELL, J. C. A., ed. The Psalms of Sir Philip Sidney and the Countess of Pembroke, A311

REPS, PAUL, ed. Zen Flesh, Zen Bones, A233

ROSE, MARTIAL, ed. The Wakefield Mystery Plays, A371

RUSSELL, BERTRAND Mysticism and Logic, A104

SANTAYANA, GEORGE Three Philosophical Poets: Lucretius, Dante, Goethe, A17